ISSUES IN
SEXUAL AND MEDICAL ETHICS

Other Books by Charles E. Curran

Christian Morality Today
A New Look at Christian Morality
Contemporary Problems in Moral Theology
Catholic Moral Theology in Dialogue
The Crisis in Priestly Ministry
*Politics, Medicine and Christian Ethics: A Dialogue
    with Paul Ramsey*
New Perspectives in Moral Theology
Dissent in and for the Church (Charles E. Curran,
    Robert E. Hunt, et al.)
*The Responsibility of Dissent: The Church and
    Academic Freedom* (John F. Hunt and Terrence R.
    Connelly with Charles E. Curran, et al.)
Absolutes in Moral Theology? (editor)
Contraception: Authority and Dissent (editor)
Themes in Fundamental Moral Theology

Issues in
Sexual and Medical Ethics

CHARLES E. CURRAN

UNIVERSITY OF NOTRE DAME PRESS
NOTRE DAME   LONDON

Library of Congress Cataloging in Publication Data

Curran, Charles E
    Issues in sexual and medical ethics

    1.   Christian ethics—Catholic authors—Addresses,
essays, lectures.   2.   Sexual ethics—addresses,
essays, lectures.   3.   Medical ethics—Addresses,
essays, lectures.   4.   Sociology, Christian
(Catholic)—Addresses, essays, lectures.   I.   Title.
BX1759.C85   241'.6   77-89767
ISBN 0-268-01141-9

To my parents
on the occasion of their
fiftieth wedding anniversary
September 10, 1977

Contents

Introduction

This book brings together previously published studies in the area of sexual and medical ethics. There are three different but very significant levels of interest in these studies. First, the questions themselves are of great importance for many individuals and for society itself. In these areas there exists much debate, discussion and disagreement today. Second, the discussion of these particular topics raises the more fundamental question of the methodology of moral theology which is employed in considering the particular content questions under consideration. Third, for the Catholic moral theologian and the Catholic believer, the credibility of the Roman Catholic Church as a moral teacher is at stake in the consideration of these questions. In the eyes of many, the Roman Catholic Church and its teaching office have lost credibility and face because of its teaching in the areas of sexual and medical ethics.

The topics addressed are arranged in three different parts. Part One considers sexual morality beginning with a consideration of marriage and divorce today and then analyzing and critiquing the recent "Declaration on Sexual Ethics" issued by the Sacred Congregation for the Doctrine of the Faith. For the past decade or so the popular media have talked and written about the sexual revolution. Perhaps aspects of this revolution have been exaggerated, but there can be no doubt about some of the changing attitudes toward human sexuality. Divorce is more frequent and acceptable in our society than in the past. The gay liberation movement is pressing not only for the abolition of all laws discriminating against homosexuals but also for acceptance of homosexuality as another form of sexual preference on a par with heterosexuality. The request will increasingly be made for the Church to accept and even bless homosexual unions. In the recent past, everyone knew what was the teaching of the Catholic Church on questions such as divorce, masturbation, homosexuality and premarital sexuality. Today both in theory and in practice there is much discussion about these matters.

Discussion about particular questions raises the deeper problem of methodology. There can be no doubt that in the last decade or so dissatisfaction with the manualistic approach to moral theology and its methodology has surfaced first and most frequently in the area of sexuality. The negative reaction to the condemnation of artificial contraception in Pope Paul's encyclical *Humanae Vitae* also signified a dissatisfaction with the methodological approach to sexual ethics employed in that document. Many Catholic theologians have criticized the older Catholic methodology for overemphasizing the procreative aspect of every sexual act and basing morality on the teleology of the sexual faculty considered apart from the person.

On the third level this poses grave problems for the Church and its credibility. By accepting and endorsing different approaches today, would the Church be admitting that its past teaching was wrong? How legitimate is it to explain such change only in terms of a historically

conscious approach which recognizes that in the changing historical realities the meaning and regulation of
human sexuality also change? Is such an explanation too
facile an attempt to explain away the previous teaching?
By accepting newer approaches is the Church merely
giving in to what is happening? Should not the Church
always serve a prophetic function and be critical of contemporary attitudes to sexuality which seem to deper-
sonalize and debase the very meaning of human sexuality?

The Pastoral Constitution on the Church in the
Modern World calls for the Church to scrutinize problems in the light of the Gospel and of human experience. Naturally there are very significant methodological questions about the proper use of the Scriptures in
moral theology. The hermeneutic problem recognizes
that the Scriptures—especially the Gospels—in the area
of moral teaching are influenced by the eschatological
expectation of the early Church and by the different
historical and cultural circumstances of the time.
Catholic theology has in theory always recognized such a
limitation in the use of the Scriptures by appealing not
only to Scripture but also to tradition to understand the
meaning of the Gospel in the present. However, the
Catholic teaching has insisted that its teaching in all
areas and in the question of sexual morality is in continuity with the teaching of the Gospel. What happens
when the Gospels are interpreted to say one thing and
human experience says another? According to sociologist Andrew M. Greeley, 73 percent of Roman
Catholics approve of remarriage after divorce. Greeley
and his colleagues recently concluded that the decline in
the Roman Catholic Church in the United States between 1963 and 1974 is linked mostly to the encyclical

letter *Humanae Vitae* of Pope Paul VI condemning artificial contraception and the connected loss of respect for papal authority.

The second part of the book discusses questions of medical ethics, an area which has been receiving increasing attention both from scholars in all branches of knowledge and from the popular media. Chapter three presents a historical development and overview of medical ethics showing the moral principles at work in the older medical ethics and the newer problems that are arising today with the consequent need for different moral approaches and methodologies. The following two chapters develop in detail two of these newer problems—human experimentation and genetics. Here again are two very significant questions which both individuals and society are now facing to some extent; moreover, in the future important decisions will have to be made concerning ramifications from developments in genetics. Both subjects point to and involve fundamental questions of what it means to be human.

Newer specific questions in biomedical ethics also entail methodological implications. A more historically conscious and self-critical attitude has characterized contemporary theological and ethical thought. Theological ethicists are more conscious of how older methodologies and approaches were influenced by the culture in which they grew up. Today the culture is rapidly changing and some of the inadequacies of older approaches become evident. However, one can never merely jettison the past, for obviously the past has attempted to deal with many of the same basic issues of the meaning of the human and has accumulated much wisdom in the process. Theological ethics, if it is to retain a critical posture, can never merely accept the present and the status quo, whatever it is.

My own biases in ethical methodology call for a recognition of the complexity of problems and the need for an adequate methodology to embrace all the significant aspects. In my judgment methodological shortcomings are most often due not to positive errors as much as to failure to consider all the necessary aspects. Thus the theological ethicist must give importance to the scriptural witness, the historical experience, the contemporary experience and the eschatological pull of the future. Theological ethics must seek wisdom from faith and reason, from philosophy and the sciences. The comparatively new questions of human experimentation and of genetics not only pose important ethical questions for individuals and society, but they also call for moral theology to critically examine its own methodological approaches.

The third level of the ecclesial or Church dimension does not appear as forcefully in this section, since the problems discussed are problems that will be more pressing in the future and are not that actual. However, the Church can ill afford to ignore these problems, for they must be addressed in the future. Too often the Church has lost credibility because it has arrived on the scene late and out of breath. Ecclesial problems and the credibility of the Church as moral teacher are now being put to the test in the older questions of medical ethics, but some aspects of these older questions will be discussed in the third part.

Part Three considers public and institutional policy aspects of sexual and medical ethics. Public policy refers to the policies of government and the state. Institutional policy refers to the way in which the Catholic Church should structure its institutions and relate to other people and to the state in a religiously and ethically pluralistic society. Chapter six considers the Catholic

Hospital Code in terms of its relationships both to individual Catholics and to non-Catholics in our society. The first aspect involves the problem of making moral directives for individuals into an institutional code, and the second concerns the code in a pluralistic society in which the hospitals are often partially financed by public monies and the patients and staff include many non-Catholics. Chapter seven discusses the perennial problem of the relationship between the freedom of the individual and the state in the context of the very modern problem of population control. The last chapter examines the popular slogan "respect for life" and discusses in particular the question of abortion from the viewpoint of appropriate public action and the influencing of legislation by those who are opposed to abortion.

Again in Part Three the three different levels of interest emerge. On the first level of particular ethical questions, some fundamental problems are raised in terms of the meaning and functioning of a pluralistic society. How does one allow for a pluralism of private institutions, such as hospitals, which follow their particular religious and ethical beliefs and yet receive public financial help and are open to serve all the people? This question strikes at the heart of the meaning and functioning of a pluralistic society which tries to preserve and foster the rights of all. The measures used by individuals to plan the size of their families have sparked a most intense debate in Roman Catholic circles, but now there is emerging an even more significant question—the means to be used by governments in controlling the size of their populations. What is the responsibility of the government and how is it to be carried out? Countries like Singapore and India have already introduced compulsory methods of limiting population. Overpopulation will continue to be a major problem facing developing countries.

It seems that every society must show respect for and protect human life. Recently the slogan "respect life" has been employed by some proponents of an amendment to the Constitution to overturn the ruling of the Supreme Court allowing abortions. Obviously the role of the state in respecting life and its attitude toward abortion are important questions. The Catholic Church and its hierarchical leadership have taken a very active role in working for an amendment to the Constitution. Should the bishops have become involved in the political process to adopt an anti-abortion amendment? Is this a wrongful meddling in political affairs? Should the bishops or the churches have nothing to say about public policy?

The second level of methodology again becomes crucially important. The Roman Catholic Church in general has had a difficult time adjusting to life in a pluralistic society. Recall that it was only at the Second Vatican Council that the Catholic Church officially accepted the teaching that the state does not have an obligation to worship God properly and to support the one, true Church. Roman Catholicism has lived most of its life in situations in which religious and ethical pluralism did not exist so that its older theological and philosophical understanding of the role of the state does not give sufficient recognition to the fact of pluralism. It was only by employing a newer methodological approach that the Second Vatican Council was able to accept the notion of religious liberty. Interestingly, at about the same time as official Catholic thought has acknowledged the reality of pluralism, other theological movements such as liberation theology are calling for an application

of the Gospel to the problems facing society in the political, economic and social orders. Problems arising from
the nature of the ethically pluralistic society in which we
live are bound to cause many tensions. There is great
need to develop a methodological approach which does
justice to all the important values involved. An attempt
to propose a more adequate methodological approach is
found in the last chapters of the book.

The third part also involves very significant questions
for the role of the Church and its credibility as a moral
teacher. The Catholic Hospital Code of Ethics has
caused serious divisions within Roman Catholicism itself
especially on the question of such sterilizing operations
as tubal ligations. Perhaps even more importantly, increasing governmental intervention in the health care
field in order to meet the needs of all people in a more
satisfactory manner occasions problems for Catholic institutions which receive various forms of public support
and yet still want to retain their own identity. In the area
of population control, the official Church teaching forbidding artificial contraception obviously has met with
great disagreement from most people in society, including Roman Catholics. Pastoral approaches can be used
to help individuals in particular situations without
changing the teaching, but in the area of public policy
such pastoral approaches are not available. I would
hope that the official Church teaching would be
changed. At the very least the Catholic Church must be
willing to recognize the enormity of the problem and try
to contribute to its amelioration in a way which ap-
preciates all the complex issues involved.

In the last few years the American Catholic bishops
have become most involved in the political process in
seeking a constitutional amendment to overturn the Supreme Court decisions allowing abortions with very few

restrictions. The bishops in November 1975 proposed a "Pastoral Plan for Pro-Life Activities" which calls not only for pro-life committees on the state, diocesan and parish levels but also, within each congressional district, for a well organized pro-life unit whose aim is essentially political and focused on the narrow goal of passing a constitutional amendment. In the 1976 presidential election there was confusion over whether the bishops were supporting one of the candidates because of a more sympathetic stand on the constitutional amendment. Some people thought the bishops should not be involved in such grass-roots political organizing. Others pointed to the acquiescence of the Church in the horrors of Nazi Germany and pointed out the need for strong prophetic protests in the name of life. What is the proper role of the Church in these circumstances?

It would be a mistake to think that the questions treated in this book are the only questions or even the most important questions in moral theology or in the life of Christians and the Church. Too often in the past questions of sexual and medical ethics have been discussed, while equally, if not more important questions of political, social and economic morality have been slighted. In no way would I want this book to contribute to the erroneous emphasis on questions of personal morality at the expense of questions of social morality. However, medical and sexual questions still remain significant and important on all the three levels mentioned above.

I gratefully express my appreciation to the following publications and publishers for permission to include in this book studies which first appeared in their publications: *Social Thought* 2 (1976), for "The Gospel and Culture: Divorce and Christian Marriage Today"; *Linacre Quarterly* 43 (1976) and 44 (1977), for "Sexual Ethics: A

Critique" and "The Catholic Hospital Code, the Catholic Believer and a Pluralistic Society"; *New Catholic World* 219 (1976), for "Medical Ethics: History and Overview"; *Duquesne Law Review* 13 (1975), for "Human Experimentation"; Fordham University Press for "Population Control: Methods and Morality," which originally appeared in *Human Life,* ed. William C. Bier, S. J. (1977). "Genetics and the Human Future" appeared in my volume *Contemporary Problems in Moral Theology* published by Fides Publishers and has been revised for this volume because the earlier volume is out of print and the subject matter is pertinent.

A special word of thanks is due all who have continued to help in my research and publishing, especially Carolyn Lee of the Theology Library of Catholic University and her associates Shirley Pototsky and David Gilson; Johann Klodzen, administrative assistant of the Department of Theology; and Joan Kunze and Patricia Whitlow for typing the manuscript.

PART ONE

Sexual Ethics

1: The Gospel and Culture: Divorce and Christian Marriage Today

Within the last few years there have been more and more discussions within the Roman Catholic Church about changing (1) the discipline that excludes divorced and remarried Catholics from participation in the Eucharist, and (2) the Church's teaching on the indissolubility of marriage.[1] The call for change recognizes developments in contemporary culture and society which are different today from what they have been in the past. Thus the particular question of the proper understanding of Christian marriage and divorce today raises the broader question of the relationship between the Gospel message and contemporary culture—a perennial question for Christianity as also illustrated in some of the subsequent studies in this book.

I. Gospel and Culture

Many times it seems that Christianity in general has seen too close an accord between the Gospel and culture. Were not Christians apparently too ready to accept the reality of slavery for many years and too slow in the last few centuries to denounce the evils of colonialism?[2] Today many people point the finger at the Christian

3

Church and accuse the Church of not standing up against the prevailing opinion and fighting for the rights of the poor, the underprivileged and the outcasts.[3] The course of history presents many examples of how the Christian Church has too easily accommodated the Gospel message to the culture of the time.

American Catholic Experience

In the United States, historical circumstances have focused the problem even more acutely for the Roman Catholic Church. As an immigrant church in the nineteenth and early twentieth centuries, the Roman Catholic Church in the United States naturally evoked suspicion on the part of many Americans because of its allegiance to Rome and its immigrant constituents. In many ways the dominant motif of the American Catholic Church was to prove both to Americans and to other Catholics that one could be both Catholic and American at one and the same time. The Catholic Church in this country tried to prove there was no basic incompatibility between Roman Catholic faith and the American culture. Signs of this approach are evident in the encouragement shown by the mainstream of American Catholicism to the immigrants to become acclimated to the new culture and to adopt the American language, customs and mores, despite the persistent appeal of some church people that Catholics would lose their faith if they became Americanized.[4] In earlier times the small Catholic minority in the United States also adopted a conformist attitude toward the prevailing cultural and social attitudes.[5]

One very significant event, in which Cardinal Gibbons, the leader of the American Church for many years, took a leading role, illustrates such an approach. The

Catholic Church in the United States, unlike the Catholic Church in many parts of the world, has not lost the support of the workers, and much credit here is due to Gibbons and the leadership of the American Church. In the 1880s the Catholic Church in this country was faced with the question of Catholic membership in the Knights of Labor. The Archbishop of Quebec had already condemned the organization and forbidden Catholics to belong. Although the Holy See had twice upheld the condemnation of the Knights of Labor by the Archbishop of Quebec, Gibbons believed the condemnation was imprudent and unnecessary. He presented his case in favor of the Knights of Labor when he was in Rome in 1887 to receive the red hat of the cardinalate. His case was so convincingly presented that ultimately his opinion prevailed.[6]

In his written presentation to Rome, Gibbons listed some of the consequences that would follow from a condemnation of the Knights. The Catholic Church would lose her reputation as a friend of the working person. There would be a great danger of pitting the Church against the political powers of the country which were defending the workers and their right to organize. One sentence in his memorandum is most revealing: "The accusation of being un-American—that is to say, alien to our national spirit—is the most powerful weapon which the enemies of the Church can employ against her."[7]

Those who espoused the cause of a basic compatibility between being Catholic and being American had to respond to attacks from two sides. On the one hand, many people in the United States, as illustrated in the Know-Nothing persecutions, were suspicious and hostile to the immigrant Roman Catholic Church.[8] This hostility was still prevalent well into the twentieth century and was apparently put to rest only with the election of a Catholic as president of the United States in 1960.

There was also opposition from Rome. In 1899 Pope Leo XIII condemned "Americanism," which called for the Church to accommodate itself not only in discipline but also in dogma to the new conditions of the times and stressed the natural and active virtues over the supernatural and passive virtues. The American bishops often pointed out that the condemnation was based primarily on a poor French translation of the life of Isaac Hecker and the condemned attitudes and teachings did not really exist in the United States.[9] However, the condemnation underlined the tension that Rome felt in fully reconciling political freedom, especially in the form of religious liberty, with the self-understanding of the Catholic Church. The problem of religious liberty was to continue to be a difficult point for Roman Catholics in the United States well into the twentieth century. It was only at the Second Vatican Council with the Declaration on Religious Liberty, which had been heavily influenced by the theological work of the American Jesuit John Courtney Murray and fervently supported by the American bishops, that the Roman Catholic Church officially accepted the concept of religious liberty.[10]

In social ethics, the policy often called Catholic Social Liberalism emerged at the time of Gibbons and continued in the mainstream of American Catholicism. In the twentieth century this policy took the form of the Church's identification with the moderately progressive forces working for the rights of workers, a living wage, social security, and even the legitimacy of strikes under certain circumstances. Problems and difficulties were recognized with the American system, but the belief in a basic compatibility between Christian teaching and the

American spirit indicated that the existing inequities and injustices could be overcome if all people of good will would cooperate.[11]

After the Second World War, as more Catholics entered the mainstream of American life and as Catholics became more generally accepted, the basic compatibility between American culture and the Catholic faith became even more solidified. Catholics proudly boasted of the vitality of the Catholic Church in this country. Catholics and other Americans were of one mind in fighting the evils of Communism. As individual Catholics climbed up the economic ladder and the Church in general grew in influence, it seems that the reforming aspect of the earlier part of the century became lost. Economically, with the assimilation of Catholics into the middle class of American society, politically, with the acceptance that came in the wake of the election and presidency of John F. Kennedy, and theologically, with the acceptance of the American issue of religious liberty at the Second Vatican Council, there was an even greater stress on compatibility between Catholicism and Americanism.

The Vietnam War and the opposition to it by a number of Catholic priests, sisters and laity made many Catholics conscious of another approach to the question of the relationship between the Gospel and American society.[12] Movements in opposition to the prevailing culture, such as the Catholic Worker Movement beginning in the 1930s,[13] had been present and quite meaningful in Roman Catholicism, but their effect on the Church as a whole was limited. The Vietnam War, urban riots, revolutionary movements at home and abroad, Watergate and other realities made many Catholics aware that there might be something other than a basic compatibility between American culture and the Gospel.

The shock for Roman Catholicism as a whole was even more rude because in the years immediately prior the accepted compatibility of Catholicism and Americanism had reached its highest point.

It would be quite wrong and inaccurate to think that American Catholics alone made this mistake. In fact, Protestant liberalism in general and liberal Protestant thought in the United States had succumbed to the same danger. In the minds of some social gospelers there was an identity between the kingdom of God and American culture and society.[14] Aspects of the theology of secularity in the 1960s suffered from the same defect.[15] Later attempts at a theology of hope and a recognition of the role of the crucifixion and of the paschal mystery have tried to overcome the defects of the too easy identification between culture and Christianity which characterized quite a bit of Christian thought in the early part of the 1960s.[16]

Also Some Compatibility

On the other hand, both Catholic theory and history show that it would be wrong to assert only a basic incompatibility between culture and the Gospel. Vatican Council II stressed the need for dialogue with culture and with the entire world. In so many areas the Catholic Church must admit that it has learned from others many important moral realities. In our contemporary world, for example, the Church has learned from others the value and importance of freedom. In our day the Church has often been taught by others the need for equality and justice for women, for nonwhites, and for other minority groups in society. One might object that in this case the Christian Church had already accommodated itself to the prevailing cultural ethos and had truly forgotten the Gospel. Such an explanation is not inaccurate, but in the culture the Church has found aspects of the Gospel which it has forgotten.

The Catholic theological tradition in theory has shown a basic openness to culture, although in practice this was not always true. The natural law tradition, from the theological perspective, acknowledged the fact that creation is good and that on the basis of creation human reason can arrive at ethical wisdom and knowledge. The Roman Catholic theological tradition never disparaged the human but saw it as positively related to the Gospel. In the now obsolete terminology of the manuals of theology, "nature" and "supernature," or faith and reason, were not opposed, but had continuities between them. Grace did not destroy nature but rather built on nature.[17] So great an appreciation did Catholic thought show for the natural, the created and the human that it could rightly be accused in part of not giving enough importance to the Gospel, redemption and faith—especially in its ethical methodology and teaching. Likewise, sacramental theory in Roman Catholicism shows that the basic human elements of bread, wine and oil are not denied but rather are accepted, integrated and transformed.

The theology of Christian marriage well illustrates that the Catholic theological tradition was open to the true and the good found in culture and did not see a basic incompatibility between the Gospel and culture. The principal thesis of Edward Schillebeeckx's volume on Christian marriage views Christian marriage as a secular reality that becomes a saving mystery.[18] Rather than deny or contradict what was found in culture, the Catholic Church has accepted it and transformed it into a saving mystery. Schillebeeckx in his historical section has probably not given enough importance to the sacred character of marriage in Greek and Roman culture,[19] but one can still accept the soundness of his conclusion. According to Schillebeeckx, it is impossible for the Christian view of human marriage and the family to be a pure datum of revelation; it is more the result of a reflective human existence illuminated by revelation. Marriage as a human commission is always closely linked to the prevailing historical realities and is subject to development. God's offer of salvation to human persons follows this human history and assumes certain characteristics which become increasingly clear with the passage of time.[20]

The history of the sacrament of marriage illustrates perhaps better than any other aspect of Catholic life how the developing human culture influenced the Christian reality of marriage. Sacramental theology itself developed over time and in dialogue with the culture. The first time that a document of the Church referred to marriage as a sacrament was at a synod in Verona in 1184.[21] It was only in the second half of the thirteenth century that theologians asserted that marriage gives a grace which positively aids in doing good. By the middle of the sixteenth century when the Council of Trent was convened it was a commonly held teaching and universally accepted by the theologians that marriage is a sacrament which gives grace and is in no way different on this point from the other sacraments.[22]

Many historical changes have occurred in the Christian understanding of marriage based on changes and developments in the culture. The essence of marriage was understood to be the contract or the consent of the spouses, which was borrowed from Roman law and differed from seeing the essence of marriage in the handing over of the daughter by the father to her husband or the sexual relationship (which was, however, recognized as being essential for the consummation of marriage).[23] Today theologians are rightly trying to see marriage primarily in terms of a covenant relationship and not as a contract.[24] The requirement that for a valid marriage Catholics must be married before a priest and two witnesses was introduced into the Church by the Council of Trent in the sixteenth century as a means to prevent the abuses of clandestine marriages.[25] The unfolding understanding of Christian marriage thus shows the influence of historical and cultural circumstances.

A Proposed Solution

Illustrations have been proposed showing there are many things in culture which are compatible with Christianity but also many things in culture which contradict the Christian Gospel. The above statement seems in keeping with the historical evidence, but in my judgment it rests primarily on strong theological justification. The relationship between the Gospel and culture has been a perennial question in Christian thought and a most difficult problem in practice. H. Richard Niebuhr describes five different models in Christian ethics for understanding the relationship between Christ and culture.[26] Niebuhr describes the two extreme positions as Christ against culture, which sees the relationship in terms of incompatibility, and the opposite extreme as the Christ of culture, which sees only continuity and even identification between the two. In the middle ground, where most Christians find themselves, there are three mediating positions: Christ above culture, Christ and culture in paradox, Christ the transformer of culture.

I approach the Christ and culture question on the basis of the stance proposed for moral theology—the basic perspective or horizon with which Christian ethics and the Christian understand reality. The Christian stance is structured by the fivefold Christian mysteries of creation, sin, incarnation, redemption and resurrection destiny.[27] This stance applied to the question of the Gospel and culture results in a nuanced approach.

Since all things are created by God, the goodness of creation is present in culture. Sin, however, affects not only the hearts of human beings but also has social and cosmic dimensions which affect culture. The incarnation indicates that in the plan of God everything truly human is to be brought into the divine plan. Redemption for the Christian has already occurred and affects all reality, but redemption does not totally eradicate the presence of sin, which will continue until the end of time. Resurrection destiny or the fullness of the eschaton lies in the future, so that the fullness of Gospel perfection will never be obtained in this world. Such a stance presents a framework within which one can approach the general question of the Gospel and culture. Culture shares in the goodness of creation, the call to participation in the divine plan, the reality of redemption and the hope of resurrection destiny. But culture also knows the finitude and limitations of created reality, the effects of sin and the limitations coming from the fact that the fullness of the eschaton is not yet here. Such an approach cannot accept either a dogmatic incompatibility between Christ and culture nor an absolute compatibility and identification between the two. The primary task for the Christian Church and the individual Christian remains the critical function of continually discerning what is compatible with the Gospel in the contemporary culture. In general, such a discerning process of the contemporary culture must be done in the light of the scriptural witness, the historical tradition and the eschatological pull of the future. The examples given in the first part of this study can be understood as illustrations of the stance and methodology just proposed.

II. Divorce and Christian Marriage Today

In the light of the proposed stance and methodology, how does one evaluate the question involving Christian marriage and divorce today? Statistics have shown the great number of Christian marriages which are ending in divorce. Surveys and polls indicate that increasing numbers of Roman Catholics do not accept the Church's teaching on the indissolubility of marriage. In general, my stance would tend to avoid the extreme opinions that the breakdown of many Catholic marriages is due only to weakness, sinfulness and selfishness or only to positive or neutral factors.

Need for Divorce

In two previous studies I have developed in great detail the reasons why the Roman Catholic Church should change its teaching on indissolubility and acknowledge the possibility of divorce and remarriage.[28] In the context of the present study it is neither necessary nor possible to repeat all the reasons which were proposed in the earlier articles. The following paragraphs will point out only the aspects in the contemporary culture and in present day theological method which call for a change in the older teaching of the Catholic Church.

Moral theology today employs a more historically conscious approach which gives greater importance to historicity, process and change and follows a more inductive methodology. The Pastoral Constitution on the Church in the Modern World employed such a methodology by beginning its consideration of different topics with a reading of the signs of the times. Christian marriage today has evolved to a personal love relationship between spouses, as opposed to the arranged marriages in older cultures which were often supported by political and economic considerations. Marriage based primarily on the love of the spouses and not arranged by parents represents a positive development, but at the same time such marriages are more fragile. Marriage can no longer be considered as the making of a contract which lasts forever but as a commitment to one another to grow in their union of love. Growth, dynamism and development of the spouses are necessary aspects of Christian marriage today. Here again one must accept the fact that such an understanding of marriage leads to the recognition that such growth might not always occur. Roman Catholic theology has traditionally acknowledged that vows are no longer obliging if the matter of the vow or the person making the vow undergoes substantial changes. The possibility of such change is much more prevalent today.

The emphasis on personalism and its effects on marriage constitute a significant moral development, but at the same time indicate that marriages might break down when that loving relationship is no longer present or possible. Influenced by personalism, contemporary moral theology recognizes that no one individual choice, no matter how important, can ever be totally identified with the person, who remains, even to oneself, a mystery. The solemn commitment of marriage requires a most mature and well thought out decision, but there still exists the possibility of a mistake which might only become apparent in the years ahead.

Other sociological changes are of great importance. The single person in contemporary society often feels alone and adrift. In an older society, within the extended family there was always a place for an aunt or an uncle, but this is not the case today. In our present American culture a twenty-five-year-old single person looking for a marriage partner meets divorced persons more often than those who have never married.

Contemporary experience argues strongly against the validity of the rational or natural law arguments proposed against divorce—the good of the spouses, the good of the children and the good of society. These reasons cannot prove the absolute indissolubility of all marriages. Historical studies have also shown a curious development in the arguments proposed by the Roman Catholic Church for the indissolubility of marriage. Before the nineteenth century the great canonists and theologians of the Church generally acknowledged that reason and the natural law do not prove the absolute indissolubility of marriage.

Roman Catholic Scripture scholars are no longer in agreement that the Scriptures forbid the possibility of divorce and remarriage. The famous exception clauses in Matthew 19:19 and 5:32 (whoever divorces his wife except for the case of *porneia*) might very well refer to some exceptions made in the early Christian community to the absolute teaching against divorce. Paul's famous exception (often interpreted by Catholics as the basis for the Pauline privilege) can be interpreted in the same way. Contemporary theology has given great attention to eschatology. Scripture scholars and theologians today recognize the influence of eschatology on the ethical teaching of Jesus. I opt for the opinion that one can partially understand some of the strenuous ethical teachings of Jesus in the Sermon on the Mount as a goal or ideal toward which the Christian must strive without always being able to attain the ideal. In the light of these and other reasons, I propose that indissolubility remains a goal and ideal for Christian marriage; but Christians, sometimes without any personal fault, are not always able to live up to that ideal. Thus the Roman Catholic Church should change its teaching on divorce.

The emphasis on historicity has occasioned a greater interest in and understanding of the historical teaching on divorce and indissolubility. Experts disagree about the historical evidence and its interpretation, but at least in some places in the early Church divorce and remarriage were allowed and tolerated, although from the tenth century there has been a solid tradition in the Roman Catholic Church in favor of the indissolubility of consummated, sacramental marriages between two baptized persons. However, there have been many other developments affecting the dissolution and invalidity of marriages.

Finally it should be pointed out that a most significant change has already occurred in the question of divorce. In practice many divorced and remarried Catholics are now fully participating in the Eucharistic celebration. Some argue that the Church should not change its teaching on divorce but only change the pastoral practice which until just recently called for divorced and remarried Catholics not to fully participate in the Eucharist. In my judgment such an approach does not go far enough. A change in the teaching on indissolubility is demanded by a proper theological interpretation of the scriptural evidence, the historical development, the contemporary experience and the eschatological pull of the future.

Strengthening the Marital Commitment

Even if the cultural and theological factors mentioned above present a total picture, the acceptance of divorce cannot be viewed as the only response or the totally adequate response of the Church. More important in the long run is the need for the Church to bring all its people to a better understanding of Christian marriage and to equip them with what is necessary for trying to live out Christian marriage in our culture. Dynamic, personalistic and more historically conscious understandings indicate that marriage requires a constant effort for spouses to deepen and grow in their loving commitment. The fragility of marriage argues not only for the acceptance of divorce in some circumstances but also calls for the Church to do everything possible to strengthen Christian marriages.

However, the factors briefly mentioned above which call for a change in the Roman Catholic Church's teaching on the indissolubility of marriage are not the only cultural factors affecting Christian marriage today. As should be expected in the light of the proposed stance, there are also elements in the culture inimical to the ideal of Christian marriage. Human shortcomings and sinfulness together with the incarnations of sin in our culture and in our societal structures also influence the breakup of many marriages. This study will now examine some areas in which contemporary culture stands in opposition to the ideal of Christian marriage. In the light of these factors it becomes even more necessary for the Church to realize the great pastoral need to create an ethos within which the living out of the reality of Christian marriage can take place.

The heart of Christian marriage and the basis of indissolubility as an ideal toward which it is incumbent for spouses to strive come from the covenant commitment of wives and husbands. Our culture and civilization have been obviously influenced by Christianity, and the tra-

ditional marriage vow or promise often used in our society well illustrates the meaning of the covenant commitment of husband and wife one to the other—"I take
you for my lawful wife or husband, to have and to hold,
from this day forward, for better, for worse, for richer,
for poorer, in sickness and in health, until death do us
part."

A moment's reflection reveals how this vow flies in the
face of some contemporary understandings. The commitment of the spouses is a commitment based on love
for the other as other—not one's qualities, accomplishments or changing attributes. If the commitment
were based on these things which can be here today and
gone tomorrow, there would be no basis for the ideal of
indissolubility. Excluded as the basis for the commitment are some things which are considered of primary
importance by many in our contemporary culture—
wealth, health and success. In so many ways the accumu-
lation of wealth and power seems to be the driving force
in a consumption-oriented society, but the simple marriage vow refuses to make this the most important reality. Health is certainly a significant value, and people go
to great lengths to protect and preserve their health; but
the marriage promises do not depend on the health of
the other. Success has become all important with many
Americans, and there is great anguish in families when
children of successful people seem to fail or even turn
their backs on the success achieved by parents; but the
marriage promise does not depend upon earthly success
as it is generally understood. The marriage promise is
made with the realization that all these things might
change without ever changing the basic commitment,
which is deeper than all these realities. One can never
romanticize the harshness of poverty, sickness and hard

times, for these are dehumanizing social conditions. But the vow of Christian marriage bears witness to the fact that these significant realities are not the most important aspects of human existence. The personal love of the spouses is stronger, deeper and more transcendent than all these other realities.

The Christian marriage vow remains a strong witness to a Christian view which recognizes that ultimate happiness is not to be found merely in the possession and acquisition of things. In our society people often feel the need for a new car every other year. It is not fashionable to dress in last year's styles. Consumerism has affected our cultural attitudes toward human sexuality, which so often becomes a quest for one conquest after another and a source of exploitation. In so many ways we are constantly striving after more and newer things, but the Christian marriage promise points to a different understanding of human beings. How often does the thirst and drive for possessions—be they material or spiritual goods—bring about a frantic and anxious groping that of necessity is bound to remain unfulfilled, no matter how much is acquired. The basic human desire is for something deeper and more profound—a personal union of love.

There is a more fundamental objection that must be discussed. Does the marriage commitment in the last analysis involve a confining limitation on the human person? The transcendence and greatness of the human person seem to chafe at the limitation of an exclusive and lifelong partnership. Do not all the boring and loveless marriages that continue to exist for other reasons also indicate the limiting aspect of marriage? Intimately connected with this is the objection based on the understanding of human freedom. If freedom is the greatness of the human person and the distinguishing aspect of human existence, then should not the person be free to enter into new relationships which might bring about greater personal development? The marriage vow can often be felt as a limitation and restriction on the freedom of the person.

Different responses to this question point to fundamental differences in the basic understanding of the human person and of human freedom. The possibility of making such a lifelong commitment of love testifies, in my judgment, to the greatness and transcendence of the human person and does not constitute an undue limitation and restriction. Part of the limitation of the human comes from the fact that we live our existence stretched out in space and time, although this limitation should not be considered only as something negative nor should space and time be dismissed as unimportant. Space and time, however, participate in a very fundamental limitation of the human. Our existence is lived out in different moments of time and in disparate spaces. We cannot physically be in two places at one time. We live in one culture, in one historical moment, in one given time—all of which are limiting factors. As people existing in time and space, we are not even sure what the morrow will bring, for it lies to a great extent beyond our control. The marriage commitment involves a sign of human transcendence because through the marital vow wife and husband overcome the limitations of time and space. One can never even be sure that the morrow will come, but the marriage commitment remains a promise to the other that no matter what happens, for better, for worse, for richer, for poorer, in sickness and in health, one thing will remain constant—the loving commitment of one for the other. The marriage promises thus do not constitute a limitation on human greatness or a restriction on human freedom but, rather, significantly witness to human transcendence because of which the restrictions of time and space can be overcome. In this perspective the reality of freedom does not consist in the ability to make different choices and decisions at any moment in time. Paul Ramsey, the Methodist theologian from Princeton, insists that Christian love does not consist primarily in doing good but in being faithful as God was faithful to his promise. Ramsey chides John A. T. Robinson, who as an Anglican believes in the sacramentality of marriage. If Robinson understands freedom to mean that at any given moment the individual is free to make a new and different choice, then Ramsey claims divorce should logically be the sacrament and not marriage.[29] The binding commitment of love ultimately shows forth the transcendence of the human and is not a restriction of basic human freedom. Nonetheless, there are many in our contemporary culture who tend to see such a commitment as a restriction of human freedom.

The Judaeo-Christian tradition has often seen the married love of husband and wife in the context of the covenant love of Yahweh for the people of Israel and of Jesus for the Church. In the Old Testament there exists a reciprocal relationship between the marital union and the covenant union of Yahweh and the people. The covenant is often described and understood in terms of the marital relationship. Yahweh is considered as the spouse of Israel in many of the prophetic writings (e.g., Is. 54:5; 50:1ff; Jer. 2; Ez. 16) and especially in the Canticle of Canticles. The infidelity of the people to the covenant is described as adultery (Ez. 16:8, Os. 4:13, 14). Reciprocally, marriage is looked upon as a covenant or alliance. Adultery and mixed marriages are con-

trasted with the covenant of God with his people (Mal.
2:10–16). In the New Testament the unconditional love
of Jesus for the Church, by which the Church is consti-
tuted, is even given by Paul as an example to those who
are married in the Lord (I Cor. 7:39 and Eph. 5:21–32).

By the covenant promise God chose a people—I will
be your God and you will be my people. The life of
Israel found ultimate meaning in terms of this alliance.
The covenant reaches its zenith in the love of Jesus for
the Church because of which he gave himself so that we
might share in the fullness of the love and life of God.
The covenant love of Yahweh for Israel and of Jesus for
the Church has four important characteristics which
should also be present in the Christian marital love of
wives and husbands.

First, God's covenant love is the source of life and joy
for the people. The people of Israel and the Church
came into existence because God in goodness chose
them and gave them life—not because of any merits,
accomplishments or works of their own, but only because of God's graciousness. Truly the gift of covenant
love is the good news, and the first response of the
people is marked by thanksgiving, praise and worship
for the gift of this covenant. The covenant meal of the
New Testament, which is the heart and center of the
sacramental life of the Church, is called the Eucharist—
the prayer of thanksgiving and praise. So, too, for
Christian spouses, their gift of love is the source of their
life and their joy. Experience tells of the need to continually recognize how the married love of the spouses
gives life and joy one to the other, for all too often the
joy which is present at the celebration of the marriage
tends to become less as time goes on.

Second, God's love is a source of hope for the people.
The life of the people of the covenant in the Old Testa-

ment was not easy. The people of Israel knew slavery, wandering, deportation and imprisonment, but the faithful people never despaired, because of their hope in the covenant. Even in the midst of oppression, bewilderment and exile they never lost hope, because of the promise. In the new covenant the power of God's love is so strong that ultimately it overcame all obstacles, even death itself. The death of Jesus from one viewpoint can be looked upon as the triumph and victory of his enemies and of the powers of darkness and sin; but from another perspective through the transforming power of the resurrection, death, evil and sin were ultimately conquered through the power of God's love. The resurrection of Jesus stands as the source of our hope that the love of God will ultimately triumph over all obstacles, sin and even death itself.

In theoretical considerations of marriage there is a danger of romanticizing and forgetting about many of the realities involved in Christian marriage. Experience reminds us all of the problems, difficulties and heartaches which are part and parcel of every marriage. No Christian should ever think that marriage exists without its exasperations and sorrows, but the covenant promise of the spouses remains the source of their mutual hope. In the midst of reverses, setbacks, sorrow and tears there always remains a hope based on the faithful love of the other. Marriage truly involves a great act of faith and of hope on the part of the spouses. The future is unknown. Obviously the future will include not only joys and laughter but also sorrows and tears, but on the basis of their mutual love spouses give each other the support and the hope necessary to face the future. Sharing in the love of Jesus for the Church, they believe that the power of their love can ultimately overcome all obstacles. Such is the meaning of the marital love of Christians as the source of their hope, so that even in the midst of sorrow there is joy, in the midst of weakness there is power, in the midst of sickness there is healing, in the midst of darkness there is light.

Third, the faithful love of Yahweh for Israel and of Jesus for the Church was also a source of forgiveness. The great characteristic of Yahweh's love is its constancy and faithfulness. No matter how often Israel refused Yahweh's love and turned its back, God was always faithful to the promise that he had made. In the New Testament the parable of the prodigal son (Lk. 15)—more properly called the parable of the merciful father—highlights once again the mercy and forgiveness of the Father which is always present, no matter how heinous the crime, provided there is now a movement toward conversion. So too in marriage the love of husband and wife must always be willing to forgive. Human frailty and weakness mean that there will always be some misunderstandings, mistakes and even offenses; but, in a willingness to forgive, the marital love of spouses shares and participates in one of the most outstanding characteristics of God's love for Israel and for the Church.

As a fourth characteristic, the love of Yahweh and of Jesus always became a source of challenge to the people of Israel and the Church. We are called to love others as God has first loved us. How often in the Scriptures we are reminded that we are to forgive others as God has first forgiven us. The love of God with its sheer willingness to give and to share is a challenge for those who receive it to show the same kind of love toward others. So, too, the love of husband and wife must accept the challenge of God's love. They must challenge one another to grow in love and deepen their marriage commitment, but above all their love must extend beyond themselves and their families to embrace those who are most in need—the poor, the outcasts and the oppressed. In the light of these four characteristics marking the love of God's covenant and called for in Christian married love, one can understand better how the marriage vow came into existence.

All Christians must admit that to put Christian love into practice is not easy. Likewise, Christian marital love calls for spouses to come out of the slavery and selfishness of Egypt and walk toward the promised land. In this imperfect world in which we live, Christian spouses will not always be able to live out the reality of their marital love. Yes, the Catholic Church must accept divorce, but even more importantly the Church must strive in every way possible to make the ideal of Christian marriage a reality for Christian people today.

Even on the level of theory and understanding, Christian love raises some problems. In the New Testament love or *agape* does not have a univocal meaning. The synoptic gospels often stress love of enemies, whereas John emphasizes love of the brethren. The synoptic gospels speak of a twofold commandment of the love of God and the love of neighbor, whereas Paul tends to avoid speaking of our love for God. These different uses of the term indicate different characteristics associated with *agape* or love.[30]

In our culture the meaning of love has often become trivialized, but there is a temptation for some theologians to so exalt the meaning of love that it seems to be opposed to, and beyond, the human. Some theologians, especially in the Lutheran and classical Protestant tradition, understand *agape* as a pure, disinterested giving which does not involve mutuality, reciprocity or the union of friendship, to say nothing of a proper love of self. Such an understanding of love from the theological perspective takes as its model God's love for the sinner, which involves the sheer gratuity of God's gracious gift and is totally independent of the attributes, characteristics or qualities of the sinner. Such an understanding of love stresses love as faithfulness and forgiveness but does not include elements of friendship, mutuality and reciprocity.[31]

The Roman Catholic theological tradition has always emphasized that God's love for human beings brings about a real change in the person and creates a true communion so that the person now begins to share in the love and life of God. The primary model of love is not that of God for the sinner but of God calling us to friendship, which mirrors the very life of the Trinitarian Godhead with its emphasis on communion, mutuality and reciprocity. The Catholic tradition has attempted, not always successfully, to unite in Christian love a love for self, a love for neighbor and a love for God. Christian love includes a proper love of self and an aspect of mutuality as well as the willingness to give and sacrifice for others.[32] It is necessary to mention this theological dispute to avoid the danger of overly simplistic understandings of Christian love. Interestingly, the traditional Catholic approach of not denying a place to love of self and to sharing in love is more open in theory to recognize at times the need for divorce and remarriage.

This study has looked at the question of divorce and Christian marriage in the context of the broader question of the relationship between the Gospel and culture. In culture, over the long run, one can expect to find elements that are both supportive of the Gospel message and other elements that are opposed to it. Reasons were briefly recalled for justifying the need for divorce and remarriage, but the major thrust of the paper was to show that there are also many elements in the contemporary culture which stand in opposition to the Christian understanding of marriage. In the light of this situation the Church must expend its pastoral efforts to create an ethos somewhat opposed to the prevailing cultural ethos, so that the ideal of Christian marriage remains a possibility. Yes, Christian theory and practice must accept the possibility of divorce, but an even greater source of challenge focuses on the need to create an atmosphere in which Christian marriage may be both understood in theory and lived in practice.

NOTES

1. For an overview of this question in different parts of the world, see two issues of the *Recherches de Science Religieuse* devoted exclusively to the question of marriage and divorce: *Recherches de Science Religieuse* 61 (1973): 483–624; 62 (1974): 7–116. Significant recent books on the American scene include: Dennis H. Doherty, *Divorce and Remarriage: Resolving a Catholic Dilemma* (St. Meinrad, Ind.: Abbey Press, 1974); Stephen J. Kelleher, *Divorce and Remarriage for Catholics?* (Garden City, N.Y.: Doubleday, 1973); *Divorce and Remarriage in the Catholic Church,* ed. Lawrence G. Wrenn (New York: Newman Press, 1973).

2. Christian Duquoc, *L'Église et le progrès* (Paris: Cerf, 1964), pp. 68–84.

3. Juan Luis Segundo, in collaboration with the staff of the Peter Faber Center in Montivideo, Uruguay, *The Community Called Church* (Maryknoll, N.Y.: Orbis Books, 1973). Segundo and collaborators have published a five-volume contemporary Catholic theology under the general title of *A Theology for Artisans of a New Humanity* (Maryknoll, N.Y.: Orbis, 1973–74).

4. "Conditions of Catholic Growth" in *American Catholic Thought on Social Questions,* ed. Aaron I. Abell (Indianapolis: Bobbs-Merrill, 1968), pp. 3–140.

5. C. Joseph Nuesse, *The Social Thought of American Catholics, 1634–1829* (Westminster, Md.: Newman, 1945).

6. Henry J. Browne, *The Catholic Church and the Knights of Labor* (Washington, D.C.: Catholic University of America Press, 1949).

7. James Cardinal Gibbons, *A Retrospect of Fifty Years* (Baltimore: John Murphy, 1916), I: 186–209.

8. Ray Allen Billington, *The Protestant Crusade, 1800–1860: A Study of the Origins of American Nativism* (Chicago: Quadrangle Books, 1964).

9. Thomas T. McAvoy, *The Americanist Heresy in Roman Catholicism, 1895–1900* (Notre Dame, Ind.: University of Notre Dame Press, 1963).

10. John Courtney Murray, *The Problem of Religious Freedom* (Westminster, Md.: Newman, 1965); Richard J. Regan, *Conflict and Consensus: Religious Freedom and the Second Vatican Council* (New York: Macmillan, 1967).

11. Aaron I. Abell, *American Catholicism and Social Action: A Search for Social Justice, 1865–1950* (Notre Dame, Ind.: University of Notre Dame Press, 1963), pp. 90–285. For the rise of Catholic social liberalism, see Robert D. Cross, *The Emergence of Liberal Catholicism in America* (Cambridge: Harvard University Press, 1958).

12. *American Catholics and Vietnam*, ed. Thomas E. Quigley (Grand Rapids, Mich.: W. B. Eerdmans, 1968).

13. William D. Miller, *A Harsh and Dreadful Love: Dorothy Day and the Catholic Worker Movement* (Garden City, N.Y.: Doubleday Image Books, 1974).

14. Lloyd J. Averill, *American Theology in the Liberal Tradition* (Philadelphia: Westminster Press, 1967).

15. David Little, "The Social Gospel Revisited," in *The Secular City Debate*, ed. Daniel Callahan (New York: Macmillan, 1966), pp. 69–76.

16. Note the progression in the thought of Jürgen Moltmann in his two important works: *The Theology of Hope* (New York: Harper and Row, 1967); *The Crucified God* (New York: Harper and Row, 1974).

17. Josef Fuchs, *Natural Law: A Theological Investigation* (New York: Sheed and Ward, 1965).

18. E. Schillebeeckx, *Marriage: Human Reality and Saving Mystery* (New York: Sheed and Ward, 1965).

19. Paul F. Palmer, "Christian Marriage: Contract or Covenant?" *Theological Studies* 33 (1972): 628–629.

20. Schillebeeckx, *Marriage*, pp. 384–385.

21. *Enchiridion Symbolorum Definitionum et Declarationum de Rebus Fidei et Morum*, ed. H. Denzinger and A. Schönmetzer, 32d ed. (Barcelona: Herder, 1963), par. n. 761.

22. Pierre Adnès, *Le Mariage* (Tournai: Desclée, 1963), pp. 91–93.

23. Ibid., pp. 76-82.

24. See Theodore Mackin, "Consummation: Of Contract or of Covenant?" *The Jurist* 32 (1973): 213-223, 330-354; also Palmer, *Theological Studies* 33 (1972): 617-665.

25. Schillebeeckx, *Marriage*, p. 365.

26. H. Richard Niebuhr, *Christ and Culture* (New York: Harper Torchbook, 1956).

27. Charles E. Curran, *New Perspectives in Moral Theology* (Notre Dame, Ind.: University of Notre Dame Press, 1976), pp. 47-86.

28. Charles E. Curran, "Divorce—From the Perspective of Moral Theology," *Canon Law Society of America: Proceedings of the Thirty-Sixth Annual Convention* (1975), pp. 1-24. See also an earlier article reviewing the literature on divorce, "Divorce: Catholic Theory and Practice in the United States," *The American Ecclesiastical Review* 168 (1974): 3-34; 75-95; also found in my *New Perspectives in Moral Theology* (Notre Dame, Ind.: University of Notre Dame Press, 1976), pp. 212-276.

29. Paul Ramsey, *Deeds and Rules in Christian Ethics* (New York: Charles Scribner's Sons, 1967), p. 46.

30. Ceslaus Spicq, *Agape in the New Testament*, 3 vols. (St. Louis: B. Herder, 1963, 1965, 1966); Victor Paul Furnish, *The Love Command in the New Testament* (Nashville: Abingdon, 1972).

31. Anders Nygren, *Agape and Eros* (New York: Harper Torchbook, 1969).

32. Martin C. D'Arcy, *The Mind and Heart of Love* (New York: Meridian Books, 1956); Jules Toner, *The Experience of Love* (Washington and Cleveland: Corpus Books, 1968).

2: Sexual Ethics: A Critique

The Sacred Congregation for the Doctrine of the Faith on January 15, 1976, officially released a "Declaration on Certain Questions Concerning Sexual Ethics," which was signed on December 29, 1975, after having been approved by the Pope.[1] A brief summary of the contents is in order, but one must study the entire statement, which is comparatively short, in order to assess it properly. After noting the unbridled exaltation of sex and a licentious hedonism in our society, the document points out that the true meaning and value of human sexuality is to be found in revelation and in the essential order of nature where one finds the immutable principles of the divine law by which God directs the universe. These absolute norms are not changed by historical and cultural circumstances, since they are based on the function and nature of the sexual faculty and act (par nn. 1–5).

The Declaration does not intend to deal with all the abuses of the sexual faculty but to repeat the Church's teaching on some particular points. Every genital act must be within the framework of marriage, so premarital sex, even when there is a firm intention to marry is morally wrong (par. n. 7). The document distinguishes between homosexuality as transitory or as definitive and

30

incurable. For the definitive homosexual, homosexual acts can never be morally justified as right; but on the pastoral level such persons must be treated with understanding and the moral culpability of their acts judged with prudence (par. n. 8). On the basis of the nature of the finality of the sexual faculty, masturbation is condemned as an intrinsically and seriously disordered act. Although psychological and sociological factors cannot contradict this judgment, psychology does help us to arrive at a more equitable judgment on moral responsibility. Psychological imbalance and habit can reduce culpability in masturbation and other matters of sexuality, but the absence of serious responsibility must not be presumed (par. n. 9).

The document points out errors that deny or minimize the reality of mortal or grave sin in sexual matters and in particular rejects false concepts based on the theory of fundamental option which assert that sin exists only in the formal refusal of God's love. The Congregation repeats the teaching that all direct violations of the sexual order are grave—the traditional teaching in the manuals that in sexual matters there is no parvity of matter. However, in sexual matters free and full consent is not as easily and readily present as in other matters. The Vatican statement ends with a recognition of the importance of the virtue of chastity by which one avoids the above-mentioned faults and also attains higher and more positive goals. Finally, the bishops are urged to make sure that this teaching is properly imparted to the faithful.

Reactions to the Vatican Declaration within the Roman Catholic Church have been somewhat predictable. National bishops' conferences and their spokespersons generally welcomed the document enthusiastically, as illustrated by the statement of Archbishop Bernardin for the bishops of the United States.[2] Some bishops' conferences, such as the German bishops,[3] while agreeing with the document, pointed out some deficiencies in it. A few individual bishops (e.g., Mugavero of Brooklyn[4] and Le Bourgeois of Autun, France[5]) issued letters which proposed the teaching in a more positive and pastoral manner. *Osservatore Romano,* the Vatican newspaper, devoted front-page articles for over two weeks to a defense of the declaration, although a few of these authors (e.g., Sardi[6] and Capone[7]) employed a much different perspective than did the Vatican Congregation. A fair assessment of theological reaction shows that the majority of those commenting on the document were negative,[8] although the Declaration received some theological support.[9] One would expect the more popular Catholic press to defend the Declaration, but notable exceptions included *The London Tablet* and the Brooklyn diocesan newspaper.[10]

I. The Context

The document must be seen and judged in the light of the broader contemporary context. On the one hand, one must readily acknowledge that in our culture there are changing attitudes toward the meaning of sexuality and of human sexual behavior. My own theological stance, based on the fivefold Christian reality of creation, sin, incarnation, redemption and resurrection destiny, as mentioned in the preceding chapter, argues for a critical approach to cultural and historical developments that avoids the error of embracing them all as good or rejecting them all as evil. There are many negative aspects in the contemporary cultural attitudes to human sexuality. In so many different ways human sexuality has been depersonalized. In a consumer-oriented society sex has often become an object of consumption and exploitation. Eroticism and exhibitionism are flagrantly proposed in our society. Forms of impersonal sex abound in our culture, whether in the pages of men's (and women's) magazines, in the mass media, in the advertising of products or in the massage parlors and adult movie houses that clutter our city streets. A narrow pursuit of pleasure, an unwillingness to accept the obligations of deeper and more profound human relationships and an inability to understand the need for discipline and true asceticism often characterize contemporary life. In the light of these and other developments many speak of a sexual revolution which has occurred in our day.

In many ways it is accurate to speak of a sexual revolution in our culture, but human sexuality throughout the course of history has not only mediated the love union of partners but has also been the occasion of exploitation, tragedy, domination and suffering. Pierre Grelot recognizes that even in the Old Testament sexuality remained a frail thing, constantly threatened and far removed from the original ideal.[11] At the same time one must acknowledge some good aspects in the contemporary approach to human sexuality. Today marriage can be much more a personal union of love than in the past and in many other cultures. Taboos and unscientific myths (e.g., damage coming to the adolescent from masturbation) have rightly been shattered. In the contemporary climate of openness (which too often goes overboard into permissiveness) there is less room for the hypocrisy which often surrounded sexuality in the past.

An understanding of the context must also consider the traditional teaching of the Catholic Church as proposed in the Declaration. There is no doubt that the

Church, as the community of those gathered around the risen Lord striving to live out the Gospel message, has much to say of importance about the meaning of human sexuality. Through revelation, tradition and the experience of Christian people throughout the ages, amid various cultures and societies, the Church can and should impart to contemporary Christians and all human beings its understanding of human sexuality.

However, the "traditional" Catholic teaching on sexuality has not been universally accepted even by many Catholics today. All realize that in the course of the historical development of Christian teaching within the Church there has come into that teaching at times a negative and pessimistic attitude toward human sexuality, as illustrated by the remarks of Gregory of Nyssa, Jerome and Augustine.[12]

There are even greater problems with the so-called traditional teachings here and now in the contemporary theological climate. The document emphasizes the same understanding of and methodological approach to sexuality as found in the encyclical *Humanae Vitae* of 1968. Many Catholics, in both theory and in practice, have been unable to accept the teaching proposed in *Humanae Vitae;* in fact, in the mind of many, the credibility of the Church as teacher in the area of human sexuality. has been seriously weakened by that encyclical. Sexuality definitely poses a problem for human society and human beings today, but there is also no doubt that sexuality poses a serious problem for the so-called traditional understanding of sexual morality as found in *Humanae Vitae* and in the present document.[13] Even those who do not agree with the above critique of the teaching found in *Humanae Vitae* must at least acknowledge that many people both within and outside the Catholic Church do react in this way.

II. Preliminary Assessment

Doctrinal and Ecclesial Authority

The first point in any assessment of the document is to understand properly the nature and authority which such a Declaration has in accord with Roman Catholic ecclesiology. This pronouncement is a declaration from the Congregation for the Doctrine of the Faith. It is not a papal pronouncement as such and hence has less doctrinal importance and significance than papal statements. Even in the area of papal pronouncements there are important differences among the various documents. About the same time as the Doctrinal Congregation issued this Declaration on Sexual Ethics, the pope issued an Apostolic Exhortation on Evangelization.[14] Very few Catholics have even heard of the papal pronouncement on evangelization, although by its very nature and length it is of greater ecclesial significance and import. Cardinal Marty of Paris pointed up the different ways in which the secular press has treated both documents;[15] on the other hand, *Osservatore Romano* has been guilty of even more overkill on the sexual document.

Documents emanating from Roman Congregations are of different kinds. A declaration—according to Francis Morrisey, who has studied the question from the juridical perspective—generally speaking does not propose anything new but merely calls to mind the traditional teaching or law as the case may be.[16] The present Declaration understands its own function merely as repeating the Church's doctrine on particular points (par. n. 6). Earlier declarations on christology and abortion had a similar purpose (e.g., Declaration on Procured Abortion, of the Congregation for the Doctrine of the Faith, November 18, 1974, par. n. 4), but they received comparatively little attention in the press and in the life of the Church.

In many ways the reaction to the encyclical *Humanae Vitae* marked a significant turning point in the Roman Catholic Church, for it was now acknowledged by many that there existed within the Church a right to dissent from authoritative, noninfallible papal teaching. In this case, a declaration of a Roman congregation is of much less doctrinal and authoritative import than a papal encyclical, although until a few years ago such decrees ended theological and practical disagreements within Roman Catholicism. Obviously Catholics must pay respectful attention to such documents, but dissent or criticism remains a possibility. The criticism that has arisen concerning this document, not only on the part of theologians but also in the popular Catholic press, indicates a sign of a greater maturity already existing within the Roman Catholic Church, even though one wishes that the negative criticism were not necessary.

The Preparation of the Document and Its Tone

Apparently this Declaration was a product of the Roman curia, with no direct input from the bishops around the world. Such a procedure is not only against the spirit of collegiality which was recognized in the Church by the Second Vatican Council, but it also prevents the document from having a greater internal authority. From many comments that followed, it seems that consultation with the bishops would definitely have resulted in a much better document. One can only hope that the bishops throughout the world strongly protest such a procedure which is ecclesiastically unacceptable and detrimental to the credibility of the Church as teacher in the world.

Mention has frequently been made of the negative and legalistic tone of the document. At the very minimum, Church authority should recognize that these documents are no longer read only by bishops, theologians and experts, but are diffused throughout the Christian community and read also by many nonbelievers. At the very least such documents must be written with the general public in mind and be seen as a way of educating and motivating both members of the Church and others.

In general, it would have been much more appropriate to discuss sexuality in terms of the basic Christian vision which affirms the goodness of sexuality and all creation, the redemptive transformation of human sexuality in the light of the mystery of Christ, but also the fragility and tragic aspect of human sexuality which is always threatened by human limitations and sinfulness. The meaning and value of human sexuality should be developed in terms of the person's openness to another human being and to a fruitful and creative life-giving love. Only after explaining the meaning and value of human sexuality should the document raise the question of the norms, criteria or laws which govern human sexuality. Laws or norms of some type are necessary, but they should not receive the first, primary and only emphasis, since norms are derived from the prior understanding and meaning of sexuality and its various values.

There exists explicit evidence within the document itself of a very negative approach to moral pedagogy. The Declaration sees the fear of sin as a very significant, if not the primary, motivating factor for the observance of the norms of human sexuality. Especially among less fervent Christians the practice of chastity has been endangered by the tendency to minimize the reality of grave sin (par. n. 10). Even more important, the tone of the pronouncement is closely connected with the moral methodology which will now be considered.

III. Critique of Methodology

The methodology employed in the document is substantially the same approach as used in the encyclical *Humanae Vitae*. The meaning of human sexuality is found in the essential order of human nature. Here one discovers the immutable principles which transcend historical categories. More especially the document reduces the essential order of sexual nature to the finality and structure of the sexual act—it is respect for its finality that insures the moral goodness of this act (par. n. 5). "This same principle... is also the basis of her traditional doctrine which states that the use of the sexual function has its true meaning and moral rectitude only in true marriage" (par. n. 5).

The faults and shortcomings of such a methodology are numerous. First, not enough attention is given to historical and cultural developments and differences. The "essential order" and "immutable principles" based on constituent elements and essential relations are contrasted with historical contingencies. These fundamental principles are described as "eternal, objective and universal" (par. n. 3). Thus, not enough importance is given to developing, historical and cultural realities. Catholic tradition itself in some ways argues against such an approach, as illustrated in the previous chapter in the developing theory of the nature of marriage (consent, handing over of the bride, a contract, a covenant?) which has definitely been affected by the historical and cultural understandings of the meaning of marriage.

Second, and in a related manner, the document mentions that human beings "discover, by the light of their own intelligence, the values innate in their nature" (par. n. 3). The Declaration sees meaning as something imbedded in human nature, which the intellect in a somewhat passive way discovers as already being there. Contemporary epistemology gives a much more active role to the human person, who positively is called to develop and to give meaning to human reality.

Third, the first two deficiencies already mentioned naturally presuppose a more deductive methodology based on the eternal, universal principles found in human nature. The Declaration cannot and does not employ the methodology of the Pastoral Constitution on the Church in the Modern World of the Second Vatican Council, which begins its consideration of each question with a reading of the signs of the times—a much more inductive methodological approach which gives greater recognition to historical and cultural developments as well as to ongoing human creativity.

Fourth, the teaching is based on the finality of the sexual act or faculty and does not give enough importance to the personal aspect. The pronouncement refers to the problem in terms of "abuses of the sexual faculty" (par. n. 6) and identifies the problem as trying to discover the true "use of the sexual faculty" (par. n. 5). However, sexual acts and faculties can never be viewed only in themselves but must be seen in terms of the person and the individual person's relationship with other persons. The Congregation for the Doctrine of the Faith cites the text from the Second Vatican Council insisting that sexual morality is based on the nature of the person and his acts (par. n. 5), but does not really adopt such a methodology in practice. As a result the methodology itself is not only inadequate but the tone is cold and impersonal. There is comparatively little mention of the relationship between love and sexuality, for sexuality is seen primarily in terms of acts, faculties and functions.

Fifth, the Declaration is guilty of physicalism, since it understands sexuality primarily, if not exclusively, in the light of the physical structure of the sexual act itself. Such a defect is clearly associated with the emphasis on the act alone and not on the person. The personal dimension of sexuality, the whole psychological aspect of human sexuality, and human sexual maturity as a goal toward which one strives are all missing. By focusing the ethical analysis unilaterally on the physical act and the faculty, there is little or no room for considerations of the psychological, the personal, the relational, the transcendent and other important aspects of human sexuality.

Sixth, an emphasis on law and on the certitude of such laws characterizes the moral approach of this pronouncement. After mentioning the values innate in human nature, the document quickly asserts that human judgments are not made according to personal whim but according to the law written by God on the human heart. This law is the divine law—eternal, objective and universal—which is accessible to our mind (par. n. 3). In the nature of human sexuality one finds fundamental "principles and norms which have absolute and immutable value" (par. n. 4).

In this methodology law becomes the primary ethical model and consideration. In my judgment there must always be a place for principles, norms and laws in the Christian life, but law is not the primary ethical model nor the most fundamental moral consideration. The model of relationality-responsibility, not the model of law and obedience, should be primary in Christian ethics. This document wrongly gives first and foremost place to considerations of laws and norms rather than speaking about the value and meaning of human sexuality in the full Christian and human context. Laws have their primary function in protecting and preserving the different moral values at stake, but the values come first. Here again the methodology employed affects the legalistic and impersonal tone of the document.

In an unnuanced manner the Declaration asserts with too great a certitude the existence of immutable, eternal and universal norms in the area of sexuality. Contemporary moral theology is rightly probing the role and function of laws in the moral life in general. The document itself seems to identify the concepts of norms, principles and laws which perhaps should be distinguished according to the degree of specificity involved. By reading laws in the nature and finality of the sexual act, the claim can more easily be made for eternal, immutable and universal laws. But if one understands law as a protector of values, then laws cannot be proposed with such certitude, for many factors come into consideration. St. Thomas Aquinas himself recognized that as one descends to more particular questions the laws more readily admit of exceptions and oblige only *ut in pluribus*.[17] Aquinas thus presupposes a sound epistemology which recognizes the difficulty of immutable, eternal and universal laws in dealing with more specific and particular questions. In addition, one can and at times should appeal to communitarian and social needs to establish the existence of laws and norms. In general, the approach of the Declaration is much too one-sided.

Seventh, the Congregation does not pay sufficient attention to the experiences of people and praxis—aspects which are being accentuated in contemporary theology. One must be careful never to absolutize contemporary experience, for a critique is always called for. But contemporary experience cannot be totally neglected or given little or no import. The lack of emphasis on experience and praxis coheres with the ahistorical and deductive approach of the document which bases its methodology primarily on the structure and finality of the sexual act itself. Without any supportive data the Vatican Declaration appeals to the magisterium and to the moral sense of the Christian people to support the contention that homosexual relations cannot be judged indulgently or even excused (par. n. 8) and that masturbation is an intrinsically and gravely disordered act. It seems to me that at the very least the last statement cannot be verified, and I would argue for the contrary.

Eighth, the use of Scripture is open to question. Contemporary theology recognizes the hermeneutic problem of first understanding what precisely was meant by the author in the times and circumstances in which the document was written and then applying this teaching to the contemporary scene with its different historical and cultural circumstances. The Scriptures cannot be treated as if they are a book containing laws which are given for all time. This approach does not deny the fact that there can be such laws and norms but only realizes the difficulty of merely asserting them on the basis of certain scriptural quotations. In this connection one must question the use of one or more scriptural quotations to prove the existence of absolute moral norms as is done by the pronouncement of the Congregation. At the very least one must do more than cite eight scriptural texts to prove that "sexual intercourse outside marriage is formally condemned" (note 16). Likewise, some Scripture scholars challenge the assertion of footnote 18 that Romans 1: 24–27 flatly condemns all homosexual actions for all people.

Eight methodological shortcomings of this Declaration have been pointed out. One can and should conclude from this that the methodology of the Declaration is not in keeping with what in my judgment is the best in Catholic theological reflection. A comparison of this approach with such representative articles on sexuality as found in *Sacramentum Mundi,* the *Lexikon für Theologie und Kirke* and the *Dizionario Enciclopedico di Teologia Morale* confirms the negative judgment and critique of the methodology employed by the Congregation.[18] The methodological approach of the Declaration does not do justice to the fullness of the Christian tradition on sexuality and tends to render that teaching less credible in the eyes of many. Yes, there are many excesses in the area of sexuality in our contemporary world and our society badly needs the light of the Gospel and human experience in order to understand better and live out the full human and Christian meaning of sexuality. Unfortunately, the Declaration is neither an adequate response to the needs of the time nor representative of the best of Catholic thought.

IV. Substantive Critique

The Declaration of the Congregation for the Doctrine of the Faith considers four substantive questions: sin and mortal sin, premarital sexuality, homosexuality, and masturbation. Since I have treated these subjects at length elsewhere, there is no need for an extended development here but only a few comments and reflections.[19]

Mortal Sin

The discussion on mortal sin and the fundamental option tends to be a caricature of what is generally accepted teaching in contemporary Roman Catholic theology and has strong roots in Thomistic thought itself.[20] The document describes the opinions of some who see mortal sin only in a formal refusal directly opposed to God's call and not in particular human acts (par. n. 10). To my knowledge no reputable Catholic theologian holds such a position because our relationship with God is mediated in and through our relationship with neighbor and self. However, as the theory of the fundamental option rightly points out, mortal sin is a much less frequent occurrence in the lives of Christians than was recognized in an older understanding of mortal sin. Why?

An older theology understood mortal sin in terms of an act against the law of God, but my theory of fundamental option sees mortal sin not primarily in terms of acts but ultimately in terms of breaking the relationship of love with God, neighbor and the world. The external act involves mortal sin only if it signifies and expresses the breaking of the fundamental relationship of love with God. Moral theology can and should describe certain acts as right or wrong, e.g., murder, adultery, lying, but one can never know just from the external act alone whether or not mortal sin is present. The fundamental option basically involves the relationship of love by which the person is linked to God. In the words of the manuals of theology mortal sin involves one's going from the state of grace to the state of sin and is not just the external act as such. The relational understanding of fundamental option recognizes that this relationship is always mediated in and through particular actions, but the external act in itself cannot be determinative of the existence of mortal sin. Mention has already been made of the poor pedagogy based on the fear of mortal sin as a motivating force for Christian people, especially less fervent ones.

In this same section (par. n. 10) the document affirms that every direct violation of the sexual order is objectively serious—the teaching that is found in the manuals of moral theology that in matters of sexuality there is no parvity of matter. It is not exact to say that according to this teaching every sin against sexuality is a mortal sin; the correct interpretation states that every act against the sexual order, even an imperfect sexual actuation, involves grave matter, but one must also consider the involvement of intellect and will before talking about grave sin.

I deny there is no parvity of matter in sexuality. At the very most, the concept of grave matter constitutes a presumptive judgment that such matter is of so great importance that it will ordinarily involve a fundamental option and break the relationship of love. In a fuller understanding of human sexuality, as contrasted with the narrow methodological approach criticized earlier, this assertion that violations of the sexual order always involve grave matter does not seem to be true. There is no other moral virtue in Christian moral theology whose violation always involves grave matter. Why should chastity and sexuality be different? For many centuries Church authorities prevented any free discussion of this question. Today many theologians rightly reject such a teaching.[21]

Premarital Sexuality

The Declaration somewhat astonishingly considers especially and almost exclusively the case in which there is a firm intention on the part of the partners to marry but the celebration of marriage is impeded. Many ministers in pastoral practice wonder much more about the vast majority of cases in which there is no firm intention to marry. According to the Congregation the requirements of the finality of sexual intercourse and human dignity call for a conjugal contract sanctioned and guaranteed by society (par. n. 7). Here again note the emphasis on the judicial notion of contract rather than the more personalistic and relational concept of marital covenant.

Ordinarily, the couple should be willing to witness to the permanent covenant of their love by a public and societal proclamation to others of their love. However, at times there might be some even legitimate reasons why the ceremony is impeded. If there is a true covenant of marital love, there does not seem to be much of a problem from a moral viewpoint, although ordinarily such a covenant of love should be publicly witnessed and proclaimed.

What about the case of those who have no intention of marriage but are living together or having sexual relations with one another? This is a phenomenon which has always occurred in human society, but at the very least is probably more acceptable and publicly acknowledged in our contemporary world. The argument is often proposed that sexual relations is a sign of their loving relationship here and now but does not necessarily entail a permanent commitment on the part of both persons. Yes, sexuality must be seen as basically something good, a vehicle of love and fulfillment; but one can never forget the fragile character of human sexuality, its effect on society and the institution of marriage as well as the possibility of sinful exploitation of one another.

This is not the place to develop a positive theology of the meaning of human sexuality, but in general sexuality should be seen in the context of a loving relationship of male and female. There is also a relationship between sexuality and the procreation of new life as the fruit of sexual love, but even within marriage there are times when procreation either cannot or should not occur. The language, signification and meaning of sexuality point to a transcending love that unites the partners. The full ideal meaning of human sexuality in my judgment is in terms of a permanent commitment of love between a man and a woman.

What about those who do not accept in theory or in practice such an understanding of the meaning and significance of human sexuality? They are not necessarily in mortal sin or excluded from the eucharistic community. There are many reasons for prudently acknowledging that in our present culture and historical circumstances the pursuit of this ideal is more difficult than before. Likewise, many people will come to the full meaning of human sexuality only through their own personal experience. Sexual relations which fall short of this moral ideal still incorporate some of the values of sexuality. These persons must be challenged to grow and to discover the full meaning and ideal of human sexuality in their own lives. Such an approach builds on and carries somewhat further the distinction mentioned in the Declaration itself on the difference between the objective order and the pastoral order. Some Catholics today—for example, Louis Beirnaert—are questioning if the contemporary situation of human sexuality really makes the ideal more difficult to attain or if these conditions have changed the very meaning of human sexuality.[22]

Homosexuality

The statement from the Congregation properly recognizes the two levels of the objective moral order and of the subjective condition of the person and also realizes there are some persons who are incurably and definitively homosexual (par. n. 8). While calling for such people to be treated with understanding and for their culpability to be judged with prudence, the document warns against morally justifying these actions (par. n. 8).

One problem with such an approach is that the incurable and definitive homosexual on the moral level is asked to live in accord with the charism of celibacy. Can one claim that such a charism is given to all definitive homosexuals? My approach for the definitive or irreversible homosexual is based on the theory of compromise which acknowledges that because of this condition, for which the individual is in no way responsible, these actions are not wrong for this individual provided there is a context of a loving commitment to another. However, this does not imply there are no ethical differences between heterosexuality and homosexuality, but for the irreversible homosexual there is no other way to achieve some basic human fulfillment as a person. Thus even on the level of the moral order, for this particular individual person in a certain sense these actions within a loving commitment are not wrong.

Masturbation

According to the document issued by the Vatican Congregation masturbation is an intrinsically and seriously disordered act (par. n. 9). I deny this assertion, which in my view comes from the poor methodological perspective from which sexuality in general and masturbation in particular are viewed in parts of the Catholic tradition and in this particular statement. Masturbation is seen primarily in terms of the physical aspect, limited to an analysis of the act apart from the person, viewed almost exclusively from the male perspective, and with too much emphasis given to the procreative aspect of the act whose importance was even further exaggerated by the poor biological knowledge of an earlier age in attaching too great significance to human semen. Individual masturbatory acts seen in the context of the person and the meaning of human sexuality do not constitute such important matter. Especially for the adolescent there is good evidence that the growth process toward the ideal of human sexuality must go through a period of adolescent masturbation. Such individual acts are not of great importance or ethical significance provided the individual is truly growing in sexual maturity and integration. To claim that masturbatory actions constitute an intrinsic and serious disorder is inaccurate from a theological viewpoint, often harmful from a psychological perspective and frequently counterproductive from a pedagogical perspective.

Are acts of masturbation then totally good and praiseworthy? No. Masturbation is generally symptomatic behavior and it is important to recognize what it is signifying. It can be symptomatic of a true inversion so that the individual is completely self-centered, or symptomatic of the fact that the divorced or separated person misses the sexual relationship of marriage, or symptomatic of the loneliness of an individual, or symptomatic of the fact that married couples are somehow or other unable to have sexual relations, or symptomatic of the sexual tension existing in a person. The reality of masturbation always falls short of the ideal meaning of human sexuality and indicates a lack of total integration of sexuality in the life of the person, but such actions very frequently are not of grave moral significance or importance in themselves. Such a nuanced judgment wants to avoid the unfortunate excesses of the past Catholic thought without, on the other hand, maintaining that such actions are always perfectly good.

In conclusion, Christians and Catholics like many others in society are searching for the true meaning of human sexuality. No one can deny the many abuses of sexuality in our culture, but at the same time the methodological approach of the Catholic tradition as incorporated in this document and in *Humanae Vitae* needs to be criticized and changed. This evaluation and critique has tried to point toward an approach to human sexuality that is more responsive to the best of the Christian and Catholic traditions and to the needs of the times, with the realization that our teaching must be constantly open to the insights of the Gospel and of human experience.

NOTES

1. The official text is: "Declaratio de quibusdam questionibus ad sexualem ethicam spectantibus," *Acta Apostolicae Sedis* 68 (1976):

77–96. The English version cited in the text according to the paragraph numbers in the official text comes from the National Catholic News Service. Pamphlet editions are available from the Publications Office of the United States Catholic Conference, 1312 Massachusetts Ave., N.W., Washington, D.C. 20005.

2. *Origins: NC Documentary Service* 5, no. 31 (January 22, 1976): 487; *Osservatore Romano,* January 24, 1976, p. 1.

3. *Herder Korrespondenz* 30 (February 1976): 88; *Osservatore Romano,* January 22, 1976, p. 1.

4. Bishop Francis Mugavero, "Pastoral Letter: The Gift of Sexuality," *Origins: NC Documentary Service* 5, no. 37 (March 4, 1976): 581–586.

5. Msgr. Armand Le Bourgeois, "A propos de quelques documents romains—Refléxions pastorales et oecuméniques," *La Documentation Catholique* 73, no. 1693 (March 7, 1976): 209–210.

6. Paolo Sardi, "Rapporti prematrimoniali e norma morale," *Osservatore Romano,* January 21, 1976, pp. 1, 2.

7. Domenico Capone, "Riflessione sui punti circa l'omosessualità," *Osservatore Romano,* January 29, 1976, pp. 1, 2.

8. The most organized and collaborative negative response came from forty-six French theologians from the area near Lyons, *Documentation Catholique* 73, no. 1692 (February 15, 1976): 181–182.

9. In addition to articles in *Osservatore Romano,* some articles in journals for priests in the ministry strongly defended the document; e.g., Ph. Delhaye, "A propos de 'Persona Humana,'" *Espirit et vie* 86 (1976): 177–186, 193–204, 225–234; John F. Harvey, "Pastoral Insights on 'Sexual Ethics,'" *Pastoral Life* 25 (April 1976): 2–8.

10. *The Tablet* 230 (January 24, 1976): 73–75; *Brooklyn Tablet,* January 22, 1976, editorial page.

11. Pierre Grelot, *Man and Wife in Scripture* (New York: Herder and Herder, 1964), p. 55.

12. Bernard Häring, "Sessualità," in *Dizionario Enciclopedico di Teologia Morale,* ed. Leandro Rossi and Ambrogio Valsecchi, 3d ed. (Rome: Edizioni Paoline, 1974), p. 997.

13. J. M. Pohier, "Les chrétiens devant les problèmes posés par la sexualité... aux chrétiens," *Le Supplément* no. 111 (1974): 490–511. There have been many attempts within Roman Catholicism to develop a more adequate sexual ethics. Of special note are two books which unfortunately cost their authors the teaching positions they held: Stephan Pfürtner, *Kirche und Sexualität* (Hamburg: Rowohlt, 1972); Ambrogio Valsecchi, *Nuove vie dell'ethica sessuale* (Brescia: Queriniana, 1972).

14. Paul VI, "Adhortatio Apostolica: 'Evangelii Nuntiandi,'" *Acta Apostolicae Sedis* 68 (1976): 5–76.

15. *La Documentation Catholique* 73, no. 1692 (February 15 1976): 180.

16. Francis G. Morrisey, *The Canonical Significance of Papal and Curial Pronouncements* (n.p.: Canon Law Society of America, n.d.), p. 10.

17. Thomas Aquinas, *Summa Theologiae*, I^{a}II^{ae}, q. 94, a. 4 and 5.

18. Johannes Gründel, "Sex" in *Sacramentum Mundi* 6, ed. K. Rahner et. al. (New York: Herder and Herder, 1970): 73–87; L. M. Weber, "Geschlechtlichkeit," in *Lexikon für Theologie und Kirche* 4, ed. J. Höfer and K. Rahner (Freiburg: Herder, 1960): 803–807; Haïing, *Dizionario Enciclopedico di Teologia Morale*, pp. 993–1006. For a recent Protestant statement on the question, see Fédération protestante de France, *La Sexualité: Pour une réflexion chrétienne* (Paris: Le Centurion-Labor et Fides, 1975).

19. Charles E. Curran, "Masturbation and Objectively Grave Matter," in *A New Look at Christian Morality* (Notre Dame, Ind.: Fides Publishers, 1968), 201–221; "Sexuality and Sin: A Current Appraisal," in *Contemporary Problems in Moral Theology* (Notre Dame, Ind.: Fides Publishers, 1970), pp. 159–188; "Dialogue with the Homophile Movement: The Morality of Homosexuality," in *Catholic Moral Theology in Dialogue* (Notre Dame, Ind.: University of Notre Dame Press, 1976), pp. 184–219.

20. H. Rieners, *Grundintention ünd sittliches Tun* (Freiburg: Herder, 1966); S. Dianich, *L'Opzione fondamentale nel pensiero di S. Tomasso* (Brescia: Morcelliana, 1968).

21. H. Kleber, *De parvitate materiae in sexto: Ein Beitrag zur Geschichte der Moral theologie* (Regensburg: Pustet, 1971).

22. Louis Beirnaert, "Difficulté d'un discours éthique: A propos d'un document sur la sexualité," *Études* 344 (January 1976): 9–16.

PART TWO

Medical Ethics

3: Medical Ethics:
History and Overview

In the last few years no branch of ethics has grown more than biomedical ethics. An increasing number of institutes, publications and colloquia testify to its popularity. Questions of medical ethics are constantly raised in our newspapers.

I. Historical Development

Such great interest in medical ethics is comparatively new. From the very beginning there have always been codes of ethics for medical practitioners, but very often these were just repeated without any type of systematic elaboration and study. Until a decade or two ago medical ethics was primarily the preserve of Roman Catholic moral theology. Catholic moral theology's interest in the area is indicated in the number of books and articles that were published by Catholic theologians.

One must appreciate how recent are the developments that have led to the present state of modern medicine. Anaesthesia, for example, was first used successfully in Boston, Massachusetts, in 1846. Without anaesthesia most modern operations would be difficult if not impossible. In our lifetime there have been dramatic break-throughs in our understanding of biology and genetics as well as in the development of medical technologies. In the area of human reproduction our knowledge until the seventeenth century was still based on thoughts existing before the time of Christ. Only little by little did science begin to understand the mystery of human reproduction, and it was only in the twentieth century that we came to know more exactly the process of conception and the time frame within which the male sperm is able to fecundate the female ovum.

Catholic authors even in the Middle Ages were interested in questions of biology and medicine. In the seventeenth and eighteenth centuries there were a few Catholic authors who wrote about modern developments in embryology and in human reproduction and about the obligations of physicians to their patients. In the nineteenth century there grew up a solid body of Catholic medical moral literature. Without exaggeration there are close to fifty volumes on various aspects of medical ethics produced in that century. Note such titles as *Moral Theology and the Medical Sciences, Pastoral Medicine, Physiological-Theological Questions, Morality and Its Relationship to Medicine and Hygiene.* This body of literature, firmly established in Roman Catholic theology in the nineteenth century, continued to flourish in the twentieth century as evidenced by the many volumes on medical ethics published by Roman Catholics in the United States right down to the early 1960s.

There is no corresponding body of medical moral literature among Protestant theologians nor even among secular moralists. The first significant work by an American Protestant was Joseph Fletcher's *Morals and Medicine,* first published in 1954. Meanwhile, the German Lutheran theologian, Helmut Thielicke, was also writing on questions of medical ethics. However, in the last decade there have been many books and articles by Protestant authors on questions of bioethics. In moral philosophy, ethicists especially in the United States showed little or no interest in content questions in general, let alone in medical moral questions, until the last decade or so. Now institutes have sprung up throughout the country to study these questions; journals exist today which deal exclusively with medical ethics; an encyclopedia of bioethics has been published; medical schools which had been indifferent and ignored medical ethics are now incorporating such courses into their curricula.

What explains this historical development? Why were Catholic moral theologians practically the only ones interested in medical ethics for so long a time? Why has the interest burgeoned so much in the last few years?

Reasons for the Interest of Roman Catholic Theology

Obviously many factors explain the historical reality of Roman Catholic interest in medical ethics, but it is possible to point out some of these influences. First, in Roman Catholic thought at its best, reason was seen as a handmaid of faith and in no way opposed to it. The great medieval universities were sponsored by the Church, which in theory boldly proclaimed that faith and reason can never contradict one another. (Unfortunately, at times in practice the Catholic Church lost its nerve and did not live up to this courageous assertion.) Many of the medieval theologians were also scientists as exemplified by Albert the Great, the teacher of Thomas Aquinas. Within the context of this ethos, Catholic theology was interested in biology and medicine and their relationship to theology and ethics.

Second, Catholic theology, unlike Protestant theology, stressed the importance and significance of works.

Theologies which emphasized faith alone would not give as much importance to the morality of particular actions. Catholic moral theology, as contrasted with Protestant theological ethics, developed a comparatively exhaustive and minute consideration of human acts in its attempt to determine the morality of human acts. Such a generic interest in human acts and their morality indicates why Catholic moral theology would develop an interest in the morality of acts connected with medicine as well as other professions.

Third, Roman Catholic moral theology from the late sixteenth century to the time of the Second Vatican Council was primarily in the service of the sacrament of penance, training ministers and penitent alike how to know which acts were sinful and to distinguish among the various types of sin. Such a narrow perspective hindered the full development of moral theology both as a guide to Christian living and as a complete, scientific understanding of the moral life. This approach, nevertheless, gave great importance to individual acts and their morality and considered the problems that would arise for people in their various professions including medicine.

Fourth, some of the early interests in medicine, especially in the case of embryology, came in the context of Catholic concern for the sacrament of baptism. Since baptism was believed necessary for salvation even of the child in the womb, the whole question of baptizing a child in the womb became a matter of both theoretical and practical importance.

Why Were Not Others as Interested?

All these factors help to explain the interest of Roman Catholic moral theology in questions of medical ethics and why by the nineteenth century there was a unique body of medical moral literature in Roman Catholic thought. But why was there not interest by other Christian theologians, philosophers and doctors themselves in medical ethics? In my judgment the answer is heavily dependent on the very nature of medicine itself. Until a comparatively few years ago the primary and only function of medicine was to help cure the individual patient. The increased knowledge and the capability of modern medicine have raised moral dilemmas and problems which did not exist in the past. Until well into the present century the primary purpose of medicine was to cure, restore to health and to care for those who were sick and dying. In this context the fundamental moral axiom was enunciated—no harm is to be done to the patient.

Ethical problems and dilemmas were comparatively few in the context of the older understanding and practice of medicine. Treatments, medicines and operations were medically justified in terms of the good of the individual patient. Conflicts between medicine and ethics rarely existed because the ultimate ethical norm was the same—a medical procedure of any type is justified if it is for the good of the individual. To justify most medical operations Roman Catholic moral theology employed the principle of totality, according to which a part could be sacrificed for the good of the whole. Since the ultimate criterion of both good medicine and of good ethics was the same, one could in a true sense accept the axiom that good medicine is good ethics. There was little or no room for conflict between medicine and ethics.

A study of the Catholic textbooks of medical ethics supports this analysis. Some significant questions such as consent, the obligation to tell the patient, and the use of ordinary and extraordinary means to preserve life were discussed; but the majority of the questions treated in Catholic medical ethics concerned questions of human reproduction. It was precisely in the area of these questions that Catholic teaching often ran into opposition from the thought of others.

The Catholic approach to human reproduction brought a tension into the question of medical ethics because according to this teaching the human sexual faculties exist not only for the good of the individual but also for the good of the species. If the sexual act, faculty and function (these were the terms of the Catholic analysis) existed only for the good of the individual, then there would be no real conflict. But the species aspect of the generative organs, according to the Catholic teaching, could not be sacrificed for the good of the individual. Thus contraception and direct sterilization were condemned. Today many Catholic theologians including myself deny such an older approach. A glance at the Catholic medical moral books indicates how much time and space was devoted to questions of reproduction.

In addition, problems also arose in the area of abortion. Here, too, the ultimate reason for the conflict was the fact that one is dealing not with merely one individual but with two. Consequently, moral dilemmas cannot be decided only in terms of the good of the mother. Obviously, these conflicts brought about by the question of abortion continue to exist today. It should also be pointed out that until a few years ago Protestants and many other people in society along with Roman Catholics also generally rejected abortion, so it was really not a burning issue.

The developing knowledge and technological capabilities of modern medical science have been the primary cause of raising many more ethical dilemmas than existed in the past. The ultimate reason for this stems from the fact that because of the possibilities of modern medicine, our problems today no longer concern only alleviating pain and restoring health to the individual, but there are many other considerations which also come into play. The remainder of this chapter will discuss the various questions being considered today and point out how they have often arisen because of developing medical and biological science and technology.

II. Problem Areas in Medical Ethics

Death and Life

Through modern technological developments medicine has at its disposal machines capable of resuscitation and of restoring circulation when breathing and the blood circulation have naturally ceased. The question therefore arises now which could not have existed previously—should one pull the plug, or refuse to use respirators in the first place even though they are readily available?

In responding to this particular question contemporary moralists have been able to learn from the Catholic theological tradition which acknowledged that one did not have to use extraordinary means to preserve human life. Extraordinary means were described as those means not commonly used in given circumstances or those means in common use which the particular individual in one's present physical, psychological or economical conditions cannot reasonably employ, or if one does employ them they give no definite hope of proportionate benefit. The basic question always has existed, but the problem has become much more acute in the light of advancing medical technology. In the past people might have been faced with the question of whether or not to undergo a painful operation without anaesthesia. Today, however, most families sooner or later will confront the question about pulling the plug or never employing the respirator in the first place.

Catholic theology has traditionally condemned euthanasia because human beings do not have full dominion over their lives. God is the creator and giver of life, and we are stewards of the gift which we have been given. In the context of modern medical developments human beings exercise much more control and power over our lives and over our deaths than ever before. Also one has to ask if there is always an absolute moral difference between acts of omission (failure to use extraordinary means) and acts of commission (positive interference to bring about death). These questions are now rightly being debated by theologians.

With the power of contemporary medical science to overcome disease and even improve the human condition, the question of the quality of human life has come to the fore. Through the alleviation of sickness, the overcoming of disease, and the prolongation of life, medicine has done much to improve the quality of human life. Through genetic engineering and manipulation even greater changes might take place in the future. Practical problems even now are existing which did not exist in the recent past. Should surgery be performed on a baby to correct a grave malfunction if the child will be severely retarded or physically deformed even if the surgery is successful?

On a more theoretical level the quality of life raises serious questions. On the basis of the quality of life, should the conclusion be drawn that some lives are more valuable than others? The basic Christian thrust admits the equal value of all, but the quality of life, if poorly employed, could be used to differentiate among various human lives. Christian and human ethics, in my judgment, under ordinary circumstances (triage being an exception) should uphold the basic equality of all human lives.

This raises the further question about the ultimate meaning and value of human life. Yes, medical science should try to overcome physical suffering, alleviate sickness and even contribute to the betterment of the individual and the race if possible, but the problem of suffering and evil must be faced on a deeper level. In speaking so much about the quality of human life, there is a great danger that our society will tend to forget about the weak, the handicapped, the aged and the poor. A very strong strand of the Christian Gospel testifies that these are the privileged persons in the kingdom of God. Ultimately, in our technological and efficiency-oriented society there is a danger of seeing the ultimate value of human life in terms of what one does, makes or accomplishes. A proper emphasis on improving the quality of human life and human existence must never lead to lessened respect for the handicapped, the retarded, the deformed, the aged, the institutionalized and all those others who are most in need of our compassion. Chapter eight will discuss in greater depth the basis, meaning and implications of respect for life.

Intimately connected with the quality of human life is the problem of the proper meaning and description of the human. The problem arises in many areas today of understanding what precisely is the normatively human. Some are proposing quantitative criteria such as a certain level of I.Q., but in my judgment such an approach

is difficult to reconcile with basic Christian understandings. In the light of newer medical technologies
new tests for determining death are being proposed.
The problem of the human is especially acute today in
the whole discussion about abortion. In our rightful
quest of improving the quality of human existence,
there is always the danger that we will write off as not
human those whom we deem too much of a burden
for themselves, or who perhaps more exactly, create too
much of a burden for us.

The Individual, Society and Others

Until a few years ago there were fewer problems in
medical ethics because the primary focus of concern was
the individual patient. Now things have changed.
Transplants illustrate how one individual can be
harmed or exposed to risks in order to help others. A
paired organ is taken from one person and given to
another in order that the second might live. Without
modern medicine the person would have died. At first
some Catholic theologians had difficulty justifying
transplants because the only accepted justification of
medical operations or mutilations (as they were called)
was the good of the individual as incorporated in the
principle of totality. But others, on the basis of charity
or an expanded version of the principle of totality, were
willing to justify transplants, especially in the case of
paired organs, provided there was no disproportionate
harm done to the donor. But most theologians agree
that there are limits to what one can do for another, and
great problems exist when the donor is a child who cannot freely and fully consent. Is the parent able to give
consent for the child in such a case?

The almost miraculous progress of contemporary

medicine would have been impossible without experimentation, but experimentation raises significant moral questions. The primary concern of the experimentor is not the good of the individual, but rather the individual is exposed to harm or risk for the good of others, or of society, or of medical progress in general. At the very minimum, informed consent on the part of the subject is required for any experimentation to be justified. The person who volunteers for medical experimentation is more than an object, for the volunteer enters in a fully human way with the scientists in the quest for greater human knowledge resulting in good for others.

The current medical moral literature abounds in discussions about the nature of informed consent and the practical ways of safeguarding it in the context of modern medicine. Above all, special problems exist for those whose freedom is limited or even nonexistent—children, prisoners, institutionalized persons. Often these people form the best control group from the viewpoint of scientific experimentation, but one must be very careful about abusing their freedom. Even though scientific progress might suffer, there are times when "no" must be said to scientific possibilities in the name of a Christian and truly human understanding of morality. Even for the average person a distinction should become more deeply ingrained in consciousness between the doctor-patient relationship which characterizes medical therapy and the researcher-subject relationship which characterizes experimentation. Not every "doctor in a white coat" is primarily interested in the good of the individual patient now being dealt with. Experimentation will be discussed more fully in chapter four.

Somewhat the same tension exists in schemes for the betterment of the human race through genetic manipu-

lation or genetic engineering as illustrated in the proposals of cloning, which is accurately described as the
xeroxing of human beings. But too often one forgets
about those who might be sacrificed in the name of
human progress. What about the mishaps and the mistakes? If one is trying to make a new type of chair, one
can readily discard the errors; but what if you are dealing with human beings? Chapter five will explore the
ethical and theological implications of genetics.

Another problem involving the individual and society
concerns the use of societal or governmental persuasion
or coercion or compulsion to force the individual to do
what is thought to be for the common good. Nazi experiments on prisoners occasioned an awakened interest in
medical ethics. The question often arises today in the
context of population control. The freedom of individuals should be protected as far as possible, but freedom is not an absolute. In theory, compulsion and coercion cannot be totally excluded, but they should be used
only as a very last resort. Especially in the problem of
population control, there is a tendency to forget that the
problem and its solution are ultimately multifaceted.
There is a temptation of easily adopting simplistic approaches which see the solution only in terms of more
and better contraception and/or sterilization and forget
about the other needed remedies. Chapter seven will
consider the questions involved in population control.

Priorities

A third area of medical ethical concerns which has
come to the fore in the light of recent technological
advances involves priorities. The question takes different forms. A few years ago a problem arose when

there were not enough dialysis machines for all those suffering from kidney failure. Whoever was put on a machine would live; without the machine one would die rather soon. Who decided? On the basis of what criteria are people given the machines? One might think that the most reasonable way of distributing scarce medical resources would involve selecting people on the basis of rational criteria, but here one enters the tricky terrain of comparing one life with another. Ordinarily, the equality of human lives should be the primary consideration. In this light of insisting that all should be equal, the fairest criterion for decision-making is based on random selection (chance) or merely on a "first come first served" basis after the medical judgment has been made.

There is a crucial problem of priorities within medicine itself, since there is only so much money, time and talent that can be invested. Sensational developments such as heart transplants attract great publicity, but should these be the number one priority of contemporary medicine? Human beings and not science should set the priorities. There is always the danger that the unusual, the esoteric and the adventurous will receive undue attention and funding. The Christian must always raise a voice in defense of the needs of the handicapped, the retarded, the institutionalized and the well and frail aging.

Of special importance in the concern over priorities is the question about the proper distribution of health care in our society. Both from the viewpoint of theory and of practice this has many significant aspects. It seems that there is a human right for every person in our society to have basic medical care. Justice, in this case, is based rather heavily on need and not on merit or the ability to pay for it. The basic minimal health care for all will naturally be different in different societies. Then there comes the very difficult problem of structuring the social system so that such fundamental health care is available for all people in our society. There are indications today that, whereas we have made gigantic strides in technology and medical advances, we have been falling behind in providing the basic medical care for our population. In addition, the astronomical cost of medical care has been a great burden on the poor and the middle class.

Human Reproduction

Within Roman Catholicism there is still continued debate about the morality of contraception and sterilization. However, there also exist much broader questions that are discussed throughout the literature on the very meaning of human reproduction. Now there is much talk of test-tube babies, artificial infecundation as well as artificial insemination, and cloning. Two extremes must be avoided. Catholic moral theology has rightly been accused, especially in medical ethics, of the danger of physicalism; that is, the tendency to identify the human moral act with the physical structure of the act. The moral and the physical aspects are not always the same. However, the physical remains a very important aspect of the human and cannot be neglected. The contemporary interest in ecology reminds us that the ambitions and pride of technological human beings have not always paid enough attention to the complicated ecological systems which exist in our physical world. In addition, the physical, as in the case of human reproduction, is also associated with many other important aspects and values such as the psychological. As chapter five will show, I will not absolutize the physical structure of human reproduction as something which is always and absolutely necessary, but I will not dismiss its significance as mere biologism. Moreover, in this whole area of artificial human reproduction there is the huge problem of the mishaps and mistakes, which has already been mentioned.   .

Ethical Questions of the Profession

An area of continuing moral concern which is often neglected in contemporary writings might properly be called the ethics of the medical profession. What is the doctor's obligation to the patient? What is the difference between the doctor's relationship to the patient and the researcher's relationship to the subject? Problems of confidentiality and the keeping of secrets often arise. What about the obligation to inform patients about the true nature of their illnesses? What about fee-splitting and ghost surgery? Why is there a lack of doctors in our contemporary society? Has intense specialization really helped or hindered the general public?

A similar set of ethical questions dealing with the profession exists for nurses. These questions include some of the more general questions mentioned above but also involve the nature of the doctor-nurse relationship as well as the nurse-patient relationship. There seems to be a temptation not only for science itself to give undue importance to the esoteric and the unusual but also for philosophers and theologians to devote a greater amount of time to such questions. As a result some of the ordinary questions faced by doctors and nurses in their everyday life are not discussed. One positive advantage of the traditional Catholic approach with its perspective of the confessional was to consider the problems faced in everyday life.

This overview has tried to situate the current discussions about medical ethics and indicate the broad range of topics under consideration as well as the general approaches to be followed. Subsequent chapters will develop some of these questions in greater detail.

4: Human Experimentation

Americans have always been fascinated by progress. Medical science and medical practice have progressed greatly in the present century and especially in the last few years. Consider, for example, the phenomenal progress in drug therapy. Three of what are now the eight major classes of prescribed therapeutic drugs were unknown thirty years ago: the antibiotics, the antihistamines and the psychoactive drugs. Two other major classes of drugs, the sulfas and the vitamins, were introduced between the two world wars. Barbiturates and hormones were discovered somewhat earlier in the century. Before this century only narcotic drugs were known; but today's representatives of this class, with the exception of morphine and codeine, are recently developed drugs.[1] The average American can readily recall the medical progress marked by heart transplants, kidney transplants and birth control pills. Life expectancy has grown because of the immunization through vaccines against diseases such as poliomyelitis, rubella, rubeola, tetanus and diptheria. Today we frequently hear about attempts to cure and prevent cancer.

Such progress could never have been attained without experimentation. Science must discover and then test every drug or experimental procedure. Despite all precautions and all prior testing on animals, there will often be elements of risk as newer developments are tried on human beings. The progress in medical science practiced today comes from such experimentation. Moreover, experimentation in many ways is a common phenomenon in our life. We experiment with our dieting, our reading and our work.

However, in the last decade or so there has been a growing realization of some ethical problems connected with medical progress through experimentation. As an aftermath of the Nazi experience, the Nuremberg code dealt with the question of medical experimentation in ten principles. The general feeling was that concentration camp atrocities were intimately connected with the Nazi philosophy and mentality and would not exist in our civilized society; but there has been a dawning recognition that there are ethical problems and difficulties with the medical experimentation that does take place in the Western world.[2]

Perhaps the first symposium on human experimentation, specifically human pharmacological experiments, was held at the meeting of the Federation of American Societies for Experimental Biology in 1948. Legal interests were sparked by a volume edited by Ladimer and Newman and published in 1963 under the auspices of the Law Medicine Institute of Boston University, then under the directorship of William J. Curran.[3] Governmental action occurred in the Kefauver-Harris amendments to the Federal Drug and Cosmetic Act (1962) and in the institutional guidelines of the Department of Health, Education and Welfare published in 1966 requiring that all applications for grants must be examined by a committee in the originating institution, which shall insure an independent determination of: (1) the rights and welfare of the individual involved, (2) the appropriateness of the methods used to secure informed consent, and (3) the risks and potential medical benefits of the investigation.[4]

Voices were also raised within the medical community itself about the ethical appropriateness of some human experimentation. In 1966 Dr. Henry K. Beecher, a professor of anesthesiology at Harvard University and himself a medical researcher, published a very influential article in the *New England Journal of Medicine* which gave summaries of twenty-two different experiments which in the author's views were not ethical or at least questionably ethical.[5] In England in 1967, Dr. M. H. Pappworth wrote *Human Guinea Pigs: Experimentation on Man* "to show that the ethical problems arising from human experimentation have become one of the cardinal issues of our times."[6]

The general public has become more aware of the problems and difficulties connected with experimental medicine through widespread publicity given various problems: the disastrous effects of thalidomide on babies in Europe; experiments in the United States in which cancer cells were injected into older patients without their consent; the experiments conducted at the Willowbrook State School in New York in which mentally retarded children were admitted to the institution at that particular time only if their parents would consent to an experimentation in which the children were infected with hepatitis (the normal units of the institute were filled at that time, but parents of prospective patients received a letter saying there were openings in this experimental unit); and the experiments at Tuskegee in which black men volunteers were not given the proper penicillin treatment for venereal disease long after it had become recognized as the standard and efficacious treatment.

The realization of ethical problems involved in human experimentations has become more widespread. In July 1974 the Congress passed a law setting up a commission of members to be known as the National Commission for the Protection of Human Subjects of Biomedical and Behavioral Research. The commission, with a two-year term, had the mandate of identifying basic ethical principles involved in biomedical research on human subjects, developing guidelines for such research and making recommendations to the Secretary of Health, Education and Welfare in these matters.[7] The National Institute of Health has been issuing proposed policy directives on the protection of human subjects and soliciting feedback from interested persons and the community at large.[8] This chapter will develop the ethical considerations of human experimentation from a number of different perspectives.

I. In the Light of Technological Progress

Medical experimentation and consequent medical progress depend heavily on science and technology, but today in our society there is no longer a naive assumption about the inevitable progress of technology. Horrendous uses of nuclear power, the recognition of the limits and finitude of human existence and the discussions of pollution and of limited resources on the earth all have contributed to a more critical approach to questions of science and technology. In reaction to an earlier naive view of human progress through technological advances, some people in our society now seem to be totally negative toward technology and its usage. Among ethicists, philosophers and theologians there are also different views about technology.

From both theological and philosophical perspectives

I cannot accept the extreme positions of either uncritical acceptance of all the possibilities that technology can accomplish or a condemnation of technology as being ultimately antihuman. Human beings are called by God to strive for a better human existence. Technology can and should help to develop and enhance the human, but it is never totally identical with the human. Briefly, technology is a limited good that must be guided and directed by the truly human perspective. Technology like any other human reality can also be abused by sinful and evil human beings. This in no way condemns technological progress in itself but rather reminds us of the dangers that might arise and also calls for a vigilance lest technological progress be put to such usage as illustrated in the medical experiments on prisoners in Nazi concentration camps. Technological progress at times seduces people into believing that human progress is always of an ongoing, forward-developing type. Today in society we realize that technological progress has not been unambiguous, but is often accompanied by increased human problems, as illustrated in the questions of pollution and of ecology.[9]

Thus in the area of medical experimentation one notes the positive aspects of medical science and technology in terms of the great advances that have been made, but also recognizes the dangers and limitations which are present. These limitations ultimately center on the fact that human beings are unable to overcome the finitude and mortality which characterize our human existence. One does not have to be a religious believer or a philosopher to recognize that science and technology will never overcome these basic limiting conditions of human existence, but this should in no way be interpreted in a defeatist way, as if technology and medical experimentation have nothing positive to contribute to human development. Medical technology must be employed in the service of the human and in terms of truly human progress in overcoming disease and improving the longevity and quality of human life, even though it can never overcome the basic creatureliness of human existence.

Human experimentation must be seen in the perspective of a proper human approach to technological progress in general, but there is one very important added factor. Human experimentation involves what properly may be called anthropo-technology, for here we are dealing with human beings.[10] There is a great difference if technology tries to improve and change what is inanimate or nonliving, but in dealing with human beings one is not working merely with an object. In all other forms of technological experimentation there is much less worry about the mistakes or mishaps which accompany any technological progress. Even here it seems that in the past we might not have given enough attention to the wastage involved, but the problem is qualitatively and significantly different when the mistakes and mishaps involve human beings. One cannot and should not take the same risk with human beings that one can take with nonliving reality. The human factor places another very significant limit on human medical experimentation. In practice there will be times when one must be willing to say "no" to medical progress in the name of the truly human. How, why, when and where this "no" should be said is a question which demands further consideration.

II. In the Light of Medical Ethics

What are the more specific issues involved in human experimentation? A tremendous interest has been shown in medical ethics in the last few years. Before that time medical ethics was mostly the preserve of Roman Catholic theologians.[11] There are many reasons explaining the contemporary interest in biomedical ethics, but perhaps the most significant is that in the contemporary situation a quite different ethical problem has emerged in medical ethics. As was briefly mentioned in the preceding chapter, medicine, as we have traditionally known it in the past, has been interested in the health of the individual patient. Good medicine in many ways could be the same thing as good morality because they both agreed that the good was determined by what was for the good of the individual patient. The first basic rule of medical morality was often formulated in these terms: no harm to the patient. The international code of medical ethics drawn up by the General Assembly of the World Medical Association in London in 1949 states categorically: "Under no circumstances is a doctor permitted to do anything that would weaken the physical or mental resistance of a human being except from strictly therapeutic or prophylactic indications imposed in the interest of his patient."[12]

As mentioned in the last chapter, even a cursory review of the older Roman Catholic manuals of medical ethics supports this understanding of a basic convergence between good medicine and good ethics.[13] The major problem areas highlighted in the medical moral literature in Roman Catholic ethics concern especially abortion and sexuality. In abortion there was another important consideration in addition to the good of the individual patient: the fetus, which for practical purposes Catholic moral theology considered to be a human being from the moment of conception. Questions of contraception and sterilization were very prominent in these Roman Catholic discussions, and here there was often a conflict between Catholic ethical teaching and medical practice (as well as the medical ethics proposed by many or most non-Catholics). If it is for the good of the person, then many doctors see no ethical problems with contraception or sterilization. Roman Catholic ethics, however, asserted that the generative organs do not exist only for the good of the individual but also for the good of the species. Insofar as such organs and functions exist for the good of the species they cannot be subordinated to the good of the individual. The conflict arose in this literature because the controlling norm was no longer what was for the good of the individual.[14] Today, many Roman Catholic theologians, including myself, disagree with such approaches in the question of contraception and sterilization.[15] Chapter six will explore more fully the theoretical and practical ramifications of dissent on these issues. These considerations show that even in Catholic medical ethics problems arose primarily in those instances in which there was some conflict between what seems to be for the good of the individual and a consideration other than the good of the individual.

Human experimentation may be understood in two different senses. In the broader sense in which the primary finality looks to the good of the individual patient, the ethical question does not involve any specifically or qualitatively new dimension, although there will always be the difficulty of making proportionate judgments between the risk involved and the good of the patient. In such cases the doctor works primarily for the good of the individual patient. Since medicine is not an exact science, experimentation is often involved, especially in the employment of any new procedure. The doctor should explain the option with its risks to the patient and obtain the patient's consent. The criterion of in formed consent has been discussed at great lengths in the literature. Problems arise in making sure that the patient comprehends enough to give truly informed consent. At the same time one must recognize the bias and prejudice which the doctor, like any human being, brings to the understanding of the facts involved and to the decision. When the patient is unable to give consent for some reason or another, then vicarious consent may be given by the closest relative or guardian. In this case the vicarious consent is based on the fact that the person who is acting for the patient does so on the basis of what is for the ultimate good of the patient involved. For the same reason consent can be presumed if the patient or a relative are not able to give consent.[16]

A newer and qualitatively different ethical dilemma arises in the case of human experimentation in which there is no direct benefit for the individual or in which the primary benefit is for medical knowledge, other human beings or the good of the human species in general. This is experimentation in the strict sense of the term, as distinguished from therapy which is primarily for the good of the individual concerned.

III. The Individual and Society

Can harm be done to a person or can a person be exposed to the risk of harm for the good of others? What is the proper understanding of the relationship between the individual and society? There are two extremes which it seems all would agree in avoiding. The first extreme would subordinate the individual to the good of society, to the extent that the good of society is said to justify the medical experimentation on individual people who are exposed without their consent to great risks, as illustrated in the Nazi experiments. Such an ethical theory would propose that morality is determined by the greatest good of the greatest number, and the individual counts just for one. Thus if there were a greater good or a greater number of people to share in the good, then the rights of the individual could be overridden.

On the opposite extreme is the position which asserts an absolute individualism which sees no morally significant relationship of the individual to others or to society and calls for no infringement on individual freedom in the name of society or the human species. Most ethical theoreticians acknowledge that at times the individual is limited by the needs of society, and society also in some ways does expose individuals to risks involving their life and limb. Individual people for many different motives voluntarily undertake jobs or professions which expose them to the risk of life and limb, more so than if they were in other professions—astronauts, circus performers, steeplejacks. In our own society, we allow people to drive automobiles at certain speeds even though we recognize that more lives would be saved if people were not allowed to drive faster than fifteen miles per hour. Ethical arguments for capital punishment, with which I disagree, acknowledge that the state can take the life of the malefactor.[17] In our society, although I again disagree with the policy, the state has the power to force people to go to war if they are not conscientiously opposed to all wars.[18] The individual soldier in war is thus exposed to a great risk to life and health.

Within these two extremes it is not enough merely to state that one has to balance off the rights of individuals and the rights of society. It is very important for one to recognize precisely how this balance should be achieved. Guido Calabresi argues that in reality we as a society do not live up to our cherished commitment to the dignity of individual human life. Accident law indicates that our commitment to life-destroying material progress and comfort is greater than our commitment to life. Why don't we make safer cars? Why don't we do away with all railroad grade crossings on our highways which take many lives each year and could be replaced but at great expense? It is really the economic values of the marketplace and not a belief in the dignity of human life which control our attitudes toward automobiles and grade crossings. This attitude sees to it that no one seems to be taking human lives and thus we can live with our "cherished" principle of the dignity of individual human life. There is the need for a quite complex structuring to enable us sometimes to sacrifice lives, but hardly ever to do it blatantly and as a society, and above all to allow this sacrifice only under quite rigorous controls.[19]

Despite some differences, Calabresi sees a usefulness in the analogy between medical experiments and the automobile. There is a genuine difference between a positive choice to subject someone to risk or to take a life, and passive acquiescence in a system that results in lives being taken when they could be saved at ascertainable costs; but Calabresi sees the difference between the two as only a psychological difference. Calabresi, on the basis of this analogy, acknowledges that the question remains of trying to find the control system in the medical experimentation field that affords an adequate balancing of present against future lives and is still efficient, indirect and self-enforcing so as to avoid clear and purposive choices to kill individuals for the collective good.[20]

I have grave difficulties with some aspects of such a presentation. The analogy with deaths caused by accidents through imperfect or faulty cars and accidents at railroad grade crossings is not appropriate. A person drives a car for reasons of one's own personal good and expediency. In the process, individuals who do this for their own good do expose themselves to certain risks. Railroad grade crossings are usually clearly marked so that the motorist is warned of their presence. Unfortunately, human error is such that a motorist occasionally fails to drive safely and accidents happen at such crossings— often fatal accidents. But in medical experimentation the question is quite different. The individual is directly exposed to risk for the good of the human species and not for his or her own good. The harm is done to the individual, and in and through this harm which is done a good is expected for others. In the case of automobile accidents, the good does not come about precisely because of the harm which is done to individuals. There is a very significant moral distinction in the way in which the risk of evil is present.

Another important ethical distinction underscores the difference between a positive and a negative obligation. Negative obligations are said to oblige always and everywhere, but positive obligations do not always require that we do everything possible for the good involved.[21] For example, the ethical understanding that lying is always wrong means that one can never tell a lie, but it does not infer that one must always tell everything that one knows. One can never commit murder, but one does not have to do everything possible to make sure that human lives are not in any way lost. In the light of this distinction, traditional natural law theory declared that the individual does not have to use extraordinary means to preserve human life, thus recognizing a right to die.[22] The acknowledgment of this difference between negative and positive obligations indicates the analogy with the grade crossings and automobiles does not seem all that applicable in the present case. One can still maintain the principle of the dignity of human life and yet realize that in some circumstances human lives will be lost. Many ethicists have described this by saying that one can never directly take innocent human life, although indirectly life may be taken, or life which is existing in an actual conflict with another life may be taken.[23] There are some difficulties with the way in which these terms have been understood, but nonetheless the general thrust of this distinction is very significant, if not always determinative.[24]

There is again a difference between what society asks of other people and what individuals can volunteer to do. There are many times when individuals can and should take risks to their own life and limb in order to be of help and service to other people. Christian ethics has always recognized the important place of charity, although debate continues to exist about the exact meaning of Christian love.[25] In this connection it is also helpful to recognize two levels of moral obligations. There are certain obligations which are incumbent upon all human beings, but above and beyond this there are certain heroic actions which we could not require of all human beings but which some would be willing to do for the sake of the neighbor in need. In these particular questions it is necessary to evaluate the proportion existing between the risks assumed and the good to be attained.

Today more and more concern is expressed about the need to protect the individual against possible invasions of dignity, privacy and freedom by society. In this context it is frequently said also about human experimentation that human beings must be treated as ends and not as means.[26] In general I accept such a formulation, but it is also necessary to nuance it. One can maintain the dignity of the individual and still recognize the complex relationships in which human beings exist with different types of coordination and subordination. Also, in human society there are human beings who perform useful functions and to that extent are in a certain sense providing means for others. The professor has a useful function for the student. The mail carrier provides a useful function for other people in society. Obviously these people are not mere objects and must always be treated as persons, but the human relationship I have with them is not necessarily an I-thou relationship. In fact, my primary concern is that such persons fulfill well their functions in society: be a good professor or a good mail carrier. However, even these "menial" or service type functions do not take away from the person of the individual who is performing them, and that person can never be treated as a mere object. In conclusion, it seems necessary to uphold the dignity of the individual human person in society. This does not deny that there are some societal values and constraints and that some human lives will be lost, but it calls for a proper ethical understanding lest the individual be unduly subordinated to the needs of the society.

IV. Primary Ethical Considerations

The existing literature on the subject of human experimentation frequently describes the primary ethical issue in terms of the need for informed consent. Informed consent implies that the individual has the competency and the autonomy to make a responsible and free decision to agree to medical experimentation. The comprehension of the risks involved and of the good to

be obtained serves as the basis for a competent and responsible moral decision by the individual. Questions
arise especially for those who are so situated that they do
not have the competency or the autonomy to make such
decisions—children, prisoners, the dying, the fetus, etc.
Such discussions often center on the exact meaning of
informed consent and what this concept implies in practice. In theory, informed consent means that the subject
knows the risks involved and can make a responsible
decision to accept these risks for a proportionate good
even though the good is not directly for the subject.
There have been many enlightening discussions in the
literature about the meaning of informed consent, both
in theory and practice. It is not necessary to review
them here.[27]

It is interesting to note that much of the discussion
about human experimentation has come from doctors
and lawyers and not from ethicists as such, but the legal
and ethical perspectives are not necessarily identical.
Recently attention has focused on the need for
guidelines or a code of ethics to be followed by researchers in such situations.[28] This raises the whole
problem of what can be expected from an ethical code
or guidelines. I believe that such guidelines are absolutely essential and important and reject the opinion of
those who say that it is sufficient to rely on the conscience of the researchers. However, there is a certain
sense in which there is truth in the statement that ultimately we must rely on the conscience of the investigator. If this is required in addition to guidelines, then
it can be properly understood.

Why are the legal and ethical perspectives not absolutely identical? One important difference is that ethics
is not only concerned with the minimal but also continues to urge an even more perfect and more human

life. Some ethical traditions acknowledge two types of ethical response—one which demands the minimum requirement of human action and one which calls for a greater degree of heroism and perfection. Law, by its very nature, tends to settle for the minimum, since it exists for the generality of persons. Also ethics involves not merely laws and norms but should include such other considerations as the moral self, with the dispositions, attitudes and virtues that should characterize the agent as well as the goals and ideals that should influence human life. There is also another limitation inherent in the very meaning of law or of guidelines. Guidelines have to be proposed in such a way that they can be understood and applied in an even-handed way in practice. Thus guidelines must be specific enough and capable of being verified in practice. For this reason, for example, it is very difficult for law to speak about such things as motives and intentions or even ethical concepts such as kindness or consideration which tend to be somewhat vague.

This difference between the ethical perspective and the perspective of guidelines or laws has ramifications in the question of human experimentation. The various guidelines and much of the writing in the field insist on the primary category of informed consent to guarantee that the individual who is experimented upon for the good of others is truly treated as a person and not as an object. However, from the ethical perspective I would not propose informed consent as the primary ethical consideration.

The active human participation of the experimental subject with the researcher in the enterprise of increasing medical knowledge and making available improved medical service to other human beings is a better description of what is taking place. The subject of ex-

perimentation is not merely an object of experimentation who has to give consent. Rather there should be
involved here a truly joint venture between two human
beings working together for the increase of human
knowledge and the ability of human beings to serve one
another. From this perspective the subject is a copar-
ticipant in the human quest for progress. This calls for a
more active role for the subject, who then truly collabo-
rates in a human way with the researcher. The subject
should be treated as a participant and not merely as a
quarry supplying the material necessary for the research.
In my judgment the concept of informed consent is the minimal legal instrumentality to insure
the possibility of human participation and collaboration in research. To fall short of this involves
a failure to respect the humanity of the individual
subject, but this remains only the floor and the minimum
for that type of human collaboration which should
occur.

The difference between an ethical perspective and a
legal perspective can be illustrated in the writings of the
philosopher Hans Jonas. Jonas points out that one
should look for subjects of medical experimentation,
where a maximum of identification, understanding and
spontaneity can be expected, that is, among the most
highly motivated, the most highly educated and the least
"captive" members of our communities. The principle
of identification, by which the subject is joined most
closely with the researcher in the human quest for medical progress, results in a rule of descending order of
permissibility, so that subjects with poorer knowledge,
motivation and freedom of decision (that means subjects
more readily available in terms of numbers and possible
manipulation), should be used more sparingly and indeed reluctantly. Thus, the larger the desired pool of

subjects becomes, the more compelling must become the countervailing justification. Jonas argues against a social utility standard based on availability and expendability and is particularly insistent on the fundamental privilege of the sick and on the danger of exploiting them.[29]

In my judgment there is something of the ideal in Jonas's proposals which cannot always be required in practice. Also a danger of elitism lurks in some of his remarks about the more intelligent and seeming to identify them with the more highly motivated. There are many reasons that might motivate one to participate in medical research. It is not necessarily the more intelligent or the more successful people in society who are the best motivated. One who has suffered from a disease or is suffering now might be much more highly motivated than one who has never suffered to that extent. In addition one cannot require the highest motivation of all people. Likewise, the sick person has both the time and availability which the well person (even the same person when well) might not have. I reject the requirement that a more countervailing justification would be always necessary to insure against the dangers of taking advantage of certain people (especially the sick). I propose an ombudsman to protect the rights of the vulnerable. If a disproportionate number of those involved in research come from hospital ward patients, then doubts at least arise about taking advantage of the vulnerability of certain people in society.

The relationship between the ethical and the legal perspectives also comes to the fore in any consideration of the legal or administrative guidelines on human experimentation. The proposed policy of the Department of Health, Education and Welfare on the protection of human subjects illustrates this problem.[30] These guidelines frequently recognize the need for ethical considerations and explicitly call for ethical competence and for ethicists to serve on boards and committees. What do these guidelines mean by ethics?

Is ethics a normative discipline or is it just descriptive? Most ethicists would argue for the normative nature of the discipline and insist that morality cannot be reduced to consensus or the will of the majority. Ethicists, however, disagree among themselves both on methodology and on substantive questions. Whoever chooses a panel of ethicists could very well manipulate the desired final outcome by choosing certain ethicists and not others to serve on the committee. As a result, it becomes almost impossible for any legal guidelines to incorporate any normative ethical methodology. In many ways the proposed guidelines of the Department of Health, Education and Welfare do not regard ethics as a normative discipline. The proposals often eliminate extreme solutions and then propose committees (a protection committee, later called a consent committee,[31] in the institution of the applicant and an ethical review board in the HEW agency with representative members of the public including clergy or ethicists and only a limited number of scientists) to make the ultimate judgments. Problems are thus solved in a formal way through a somewhat representative committee.

This is probably the only way in which such guidelines can function in our pluralistic society. Even in ethical theory there is a validity to the disinterested person making judgments and using as a criterion whether or not one would subject one's own children to such experiments. However, I would urge that the people who serve on these boards and the researchers themselves should acquaint themselves with the various ethical considerations and their implications for these questions of experimentation.

Informed consent is a very essential aspect of the par-

ticipation of the subject in experimental research, but
consent alone is not the only important ethical aspect.
Even the usual treatments of informed consent recognize that this is a means so that the individual can make
the judgment about the proportionality between the
risks and the good to be obtained. The researcher before proposing research must also make such judgments. What this indicates is that from the ethical
viewpoint the freedom of the subject is not the only
question involved. According to my understanding of
ethical theory, freedom cannot be the only ethical consideration.[32] There are certain things which are ethically
wrong (e.g., sadistic relationships), and free consent
does not make them ethically right. In this case at the
very least there must be a reasonable proportionality
between the risks involved and the goal to be sought.
There is much need to discuss this question of proportionate reason in justifying the risks involved in human
experimentation, for it concerns both the researcher in
proposing the research and also the subject in consent-
ing to it.

V. Practical Obstacles

It is now necessary to consider the practical obstacles
or conflicts which in reality may inhibit the subject from
fully participating and collaborating in a human way in
the experimentation. The ultimate source of conflict
comes from the fact that the researcher is interested
primarily in the knowledge to be obtained from the experiment and not in the good of the individual. This
basic source of conflict is accentuated by the fact that in
the eyes of most people there is no distinction between
the physician and the researcher.

First of all, it is necessary for the patient to recognize the distinction between the researcher and the physician even if it might happen to be one and the same person who exercises both functions. Traditionally, the doctor has enjoyed a very high position of trust in our society. The patient generally looks upon the physician as the one who is able to cure and help when one is sick and ailing. The average patient tends to think that all people in white coats are doctors and is predisposed to agree with everything that is asked of them by the "doctor."[33]

Obviously education of all types is necessary so that the general society is able to distinguish the two roles involved. However, an ability to intellectually distinguish the two roles is not sufficient. Many other subtle forms of pressure and coercion exist. To alleviate some of these forms of pressure especially as they exist in hospital situations different suggestions have been made. Otto Guttentag concludes his study of human experimentation by making the practical recommendation that experiments done not for the immediate good of the individual subject but for the welfare of others should be performed by experimentors who are not simultaneously responsible for the clinical care of the individual. Such a system of checks and balances exists in practice today in the question of heart transplants with the death of the donor certified by doctors who are not involved with the intended recipient of the heart.[34]

John Fletcher, a Christian ethicist who has devoted much study to the practical aspects of informed consent, wants research institutions to act on Guttentag's suggestion. Fletcher mentions three factors which can affect and limit the autonomy of patients—the very fact of being ill, the circumstances surrounding the institution itself, and the desire to please the investigator. All medical institutions engaging in human experimentation should designate one or more persons as an advocate or ombudsman for the patient [35] I agree that the work of an ombudsman safeguards in practice the individual when there are forms of pressure which can affect the autonomy and competency to give informed consent.

Practical ethical analysis has the task to discern the pressures which are involved in situations and to act against them. *Agere contra* has been a traditionally accepted norm in ethics and in spiritual theology. Another form of pressure comes from the competition existing within the field of research—something which is not necessarily bad in itself. Awards and recognition often go to the first one to make a medical break-through, but the desire to be first might tempt one to act hastily and disregard certain ethical aspects of a situation. This type of competition causes problems on all levels of medical research. Two empirical studies done by Barber and associates point up the problem of competition of researchers for academic rank and prominence, even on a local level within a given institution. Their data show that "those who have been less rewarded by local rank than peers for whatever they have performed in the area they have emphasized are more likely to be led to take advantage of human subjects in order to increase their chances of promotion by publishing significant scientific work."[36]

As mentioned earlier, ethical guidelines alone are not enough and it is necessary to rely on the conscientious convictions of researchers themselves. However, the studies by Barber et al. indicate that researchers themselves do not give a very high priority for emphasis on ethical concerns. Much medical experimentation is done in collaboration, but how desirable is the characteristic of ethical sensitivity of a fellow collaborator? The studies by Barber et al. indicate that the climate of biomedical research groups is more favorable to the position designated as "value of research" than it is to the "humane therapy" position. Their data indicates that while characteristics of researchers such as "scientific ability" and "motivation to work hard" are highly desirable in choosing collaborators, "ethical concerns for research subjects" is at the other extreme of salience.[37] Granted the limited studies involved, nonetheless, it seems that there is a great need to change the climate in which human experimentation takes place. Responsibility here seems to fall primarily on medical schools and on the medical community itself.[38] It is necessary to acquaint researchers from the very beginning with the ethical problems which can and often do arise.

Other forms of pressure would include that existing when medical professors ask their students to participate in medical experimentation. Likewise, in university hospitals the residents are under pressure to cooperate with senior professors who want to use the residents' patients for research because the residents are dependent upon the senior staff in many ways for help and advice. This section has not attempted an exhaustive discernment of all the pressures which can exist, but merely indicates some of these pressures to highlight the need to be continually vigilant against the different types of pressures existing and to realize the need to act against them in an attempt to neutralize them.

VI. Experimentation Involving Children

As a final section it will be helpful to discuss in more detail a significant and prismatic case—the use of children in nontherapeutic experimentation. Again the discussion will not descend to the level of proposing guidelines, so, for example, it will not even discuss the exact age of what is meant by children who are unable to give consent.

There has been a great divergence in the literature and proposed guidelines about the ethics of using children in medical experimentation understood in the strict sense. Many researchers have proposed the need to use children but also recognized the role of proper safeguards. Louis Lasagna, a professor of medicine and experimental therapeutics, accepts the use of children and even justifies the famous experiment at the Willowbrook School in New York.[39] Franz J. Ingelfinger, an editor of the *New England Journal of Medicine,* argues against the absolute position of the World Medical Association statement that will not allow experimentation on children under any circumstances.[40] Charles Lowe, M.D., and associates point out all the advantages that have accrued through experimentation on children and conclude to its necessity but recognize the need for some ethical restrictions which very well might prevent our obtaining some of the knowledge and technological progress which we did obtain in the past.[41] The proposed HEW guidelines also begin with the assumption that experimentation on children is necessary for medical advances for the good of other children. These guidelines conclude that substantial risk with children is never acceptable but that some risk is justified with the ultimate determination made by review committees.[42]

Not all researchers have proposed that the parents can consent to research on their children. Henry K. Beecher and William J. Curran conclude that children under 14 may be involved in medical experimentation only when there is no discernible risk.[43] As might be expected, some philosophical and religious ethicists tend to be more reluctant or even opposed to the use of children in medical experimentation, but again this does not hold true of all ethicists. Paul Ramsey, based on the canon of loyalty by which the parent is related to the child, opposes any medical experimentation with children because the primary ethical consideration is not the risk or degree of risk but the offense of touching which would be involved in any experimentation.[44] William E. May supports the same conclusion, since proxy consent by the parents in such cases involves a contradiction—it necessarily requires one to treat a child or other incompetent individual as a moral agent, something that a child or other incompetent actually is not.[45]

Richard A. McCormick has disagreed with Ramsey and come to a conclusion similar to Beecher's in allowing experimentation where there is no discernible risk (although he at times speaks of no notable disadvantages and accepts the concept of low risk if it means no realistic risk), undue discomfort or inconvenience.[46] McCormick bases his conclusion on the fact that such an act is something that one ought to do for other members of the human community and is not merely a work of charity or of supererogation which would never be justified by proxy consent. Elsewhere McCormick rightly points out that his conclusion is quite similar to the one I have proposed on this question.[47]

In the light of further considerations I have changed my earlier position, which in reaction to Paul Ramsey's approach proposed that experimentation on children is acceptable when there is no discernible risk.[48] Now I am willing to accept some risk, discomfort or inconvenience.

McCormick and others claim that the HEW guidelines are utilitarian, but I do not think that conclusion is necessarily accurate. Unlike McCormick, I would see the individual human being in more relational terms rather than as an individual with certain basic human tendencies or human goods which are equally basic and self-evidently attractive and against which one must never directly choose.[49] A more relational understanding would not see all these goods as equally basic and of equal value. Likewise without unduly subordinating the individual to society or others, this view recognizes that in our relational existence with others we are often exposed to some risk which is not for our benefit, even in the case of children. In a less complex and relational world a child would be better off growing up in an environment where there is no air pollution, but other values are decisive in the choice of where the family lives even though this redounds only secondarily to the good of the child and definitely causes some harm to the child. One might argue that even here the decision is made for the good of the child, but consider another example. I believe that individual children in some circumstances should undergo the inconvenience of busing in order to achieve racial integration of schools—which is proximately and primarily for the good of others and only very indirectly redounds to the good of the individual child.

A more relational understanding recognizes that often children are exposed by parents and others to some risk or inconvenience which is not primarily and directly for their own benefit. I agree with McCormick and Lowe and associates that it is necessary here to distinguish two kinds of obligations.[50] A person could freely expose oneself to a greater risk than the parent can take with the child. The parent can however expose the child to some risk, low risk or slight risk for the good of others. My primary difficulty with the HEW guidelines is the failure to spell out what is meant by some risk which is permitted, as opposed to substantial risk which is forbidden. As practical guidelines these would be much more helpful and less open to abuse if they would offer a more explicit understanding of what is meant by some risk and thereby give more detailed guidelines for the final decision to be made by review committees.

Although I would accept the ethical validity of parents giving proxy consent for experimentation which exposes their child to low risk, some risk or slight risk (or discomfort or inconvenience), I still recognize the absolute need for practical vigilance in all areas of such experimentation. Above all, children should never be used in experimentation unless there is no other way to achieve the purpose of the experiment.

The Ramsey-McCormick discussion has continued.[51] McCormick characterizes Ramsey's position of allowing no experimentation on children as narrowly individualistic and denying the social nature of all human beings. McCormick still holds for allowing parents to consent to experimentation on children if there is no discernible risk, or minimal risk or no notable inconvenience.

It is interesting that McCormick employs the same basic argument against Ramsey which I have used against his own position. The differences between us can be reduced to three areas. First, I would allow consent for experimentation on children in some cases where there is some or slight risk, as distinguished from no discernible risk on one hand or significant risk on the other. Is it ever possible to meet the criterion of no discernible risk? Perhaps in practice the difference between us is not that great. There is need to spell out exactly what we mean by these different terms. Second, my position gives more significance to the social aspect of human existence by saying that exposure at times to some or slight risk is a part of our social nature. Third, McCormick's ethical theory based on DeFinance, Grisez and Finnis still appears too individualistic because it rests on a concept of the individual person and one's basic tendencies. I would make the multiple relationship aspect of human existence more basic.

VII. Conclusion

Interest in and discussion about experimentation with human subjects continues and will even be intensified in the immediate future. As mentioned above, in November 1973, the Director of the National Institutes of Health first published in the *Federal Register* draft proposals providing for the protection of human subjects involved in research, development or related activities supported by grants or contracts from the Department of Health, Education and Welfare (HEW). At that time it was indicated that regulations would be developed concerning minors, fetuses, abortuses, prisoners and the institutionalized mentally disabled.[52] Dialogue about these proposals and further drafting continued. Such regulations governing all grants from HEW will obviously set the standards for practically all medical research and experimentation in the United States.

In July 1974, Congress passed the "National Research Act," and the President signed P.L. 93-348 into law. Among other things, this law established a National Commission for the Protection of Human Subjects in Biomedical and Behavioral Research. The Commission was mandated to make reports and recommendations of ethical guidelines for the conduct of research supported by HEW. In addition, the Commission should make recommendations to Congress regarding the protection of human subjects in research not subject to regulation by HEW.[53]

This present study has attempted to contribute to the ongoing dialogue by giving an overall perspective of the ethical considerations of human experimentation without descending into the particulars which should characterize guidelines and without an exhaustive discussion of all the possible cases in which competency or autonomy or both are affected. The primary consideration involves the proper relationship of the individual to society. The rights of the individual mean that at times one must say "no" to proposed experimentation. In the case of children, since the child has some ordering to others and to society, I would justify the proxy consent of parents to experiments if the risk for the child is slight or low.

NOTES

1. Bernard Barber et al., *Research on Human Subjects* (New York: Russell Sage Foundation, 1973), p. 1.

2. For an exhaustive study on the subject of human experimentation, including the most important codes and summaries of the most significant cases and articles, see Jay Katz, *Experimentation with Human Beings* (New York: Russell Sage Foundation, 1972).

3. *Clinical Investigation in Medicine,* ed. Ladimer and Newman (Boston: Boston University Law-Medicine Research Institute, 1963).

4. Cited by Henry K. Beecher, *Research and the Individual* (Boston: Little, Brown and Co., 1970), p. 293. Beecher's book is a thorough treatment of the question and includes a helpful appendix containing in chronological order the various codes referring to experimentation.

5. Henry K. Beecher, "Ethics and Clinical Research," *New England Journal of Medicine* 274 (1966): 1354–1360.

6. M. H. Pappworth, *Human Guinea Pigs: Experimentation on Man* (London: Routledge and Kegan Paul Ltd., 1967).

7. Public Health Service Act, 42 U.S.C.A. § 289*l*-1, Historical Note (1974).

8. Proposed HEW Reg., "Protection of Human Subjects," *Federal Register* 38 (1973): 31738.

9. For a generally convincing exposition, which occasionally might be too optimistic, see Victor C. Ferkiss, *Technological Man: The Myth and the Reality* (New York: New American Library, 1970).

10. August-Wilhelm von Eiff and Franz Böckle, "Experimentation in Clinical Research," *Concilium* 65 (May 1971): 80.

11. LeRoy Walters, "Medical Ethics," *New Catholic Encyclopedia Supplement* 16, pp. 290-291.

12. Beecher, *Research and the Individual*, p. 236.

13. Representative of this type of literature are the following: Edwin F. Healy, *Medical Ethics* (Chicago: Loyola University Press, 1956); Gerald Kelly, *Medico-Moral Problems* (St. Louis: Catholic Hospital Association, 1958); Charles J. McFadden, *Medical Ethics*, 6th ed. (Philadelphia: F. A. Davis, 1967); Thomas J. O'Donnell, *Morals in Medicine* (Westminster, Md.: Newman Press, 1956). For recent books by Protestant ethicists on medical ethics which include sections on experimentation, see Paul Ramsey, *The Patient as Person* (New Haven: Yale University Press, 1970); Harmon L. Smith, *Ethics and the New Medicine* (Nashville: Abingdon, 1970); James B. Nelson, *Human Medicine* (Minneapolis: Augsburg Publishing House, 1973).

14. John C. Ford and Gerald Kelly, *Contemporary Moral Theology*, vol. II: *Marriage Questions* (Westminster, Md.: Newman Press, 1963), pp. 235-459.

15. Charles E. Curran, *New Perspectives in Moral Theology* (Notre Dame, Ind.: University of Notre Dame Press, 1976), pp. 194-211.

16. Thomas J. O'Donnell, "Informed Consent," *Journal of the American Medical Association* 277 (1974): 73.

17. For a refutation of the traditional justification of capital punishment in the Catholic tradition, see Norman St. John-Stevas, *The Right to Life* (Holt, Rinehart and Winston, 1964), pp. 80-102.

18. Charles E. Curran, *Politics, Medicine and Christian Ethics: A Dialogue with Paul Ramsey* (Philadelphia: Fortress Press, 1973), pp. 101-109.

19. Guido Calabresi, "Reflections on Medical Experimentation in Humans," in *Experimentation with Human Subjects*, ed. Paul A. Freund (New York: G. Braziller, 1970), pp. 178-182.

20. Ibid., pp. 183-184.

21. H. Noldin et al., *Summa Theologiae Moralis*, vol. I: *De Principiis*, 33d ed. (Innsbruck: Rauch, 1960), pp. 166-169.

22. Daniel A. Cronin, *The Moral Law in Regard to the Ordinary and Extraordinary Means of Conserving Life* (Rome: Gregorian University Press, 1958), pp. 32-45.

23. Paul Ramsey, "Abortion: A Review Article," *The Thomist* 37 (1973): 212ff.

24. For recent surveys and evaluations of a growing literature on this subject, see Leandro Rossi, "Il limite del principio del duplice effeto," *Rivista di Teologia Morale* 13 (1972): 11–37; Richard A. McCormick, *Ambiguity in Moral Choice* (Milwaukee: Marquette University, 1973).

25. For a recent work, see Gene Outka, *Agape: An Ethical Analysis* (New Haven: Yale University Press, 1972).

26. Edward Shils, "Social Inquiry and the Autonomy of the Individual," in *The Human Meaning of the Social Sciences*, ed. Daniel Lerner (Cleveland: Meridian Books, 1959), pp. 114–157.

27. The most significant books are by Katz and Beecher as well as the volume edited by Freund.

28. See Public Health Service Act, 42 U.S.C.A. § 289*l*-1, Historical Note (1974).

29. Hans Jonas, "Philosophical Reflections on Experimenting with Human Subjects," in *Experimentation with Human Subjects*, pp. 18–22.

30. Proposed HEW Reg., "Protection of Human Subjects," *Federal Register* 38 (1973): 31738–31748; 39 (1974): 30648–30657.

31. *Federal Register* 39 (1974): 30650.

32. John McNeill, "Freedom and the Future," *Theological Studies* 33 (1972): 503–530.

33. George A. Kanoti, "A New Priesthood?" *The Linacre Quarterly* 39 (1972): 193–198.

34. Otto E. Guttentag, "Ethical Problems in Human Experimentation," in *Ethical Issues in Medicine*, ed. E. Fuller Torrey (Boston: Little, Brown and Co., 1968), pp. 212, 213.

35. John Fletcher, "Realities of Patient Consent to Medical Research," *Hastings Center Studies* 1, no. 1 (1973): 39–49.

36. Barber et al., *Research on Human Subjects*, p. 91.

37. Ibid., p. 192.

38. Julia Loughlin Makarushka and John J. Lally, "Medical Schools, Clinical Research and Leadership," *Journal of Medical Education* 49 (1974): 416.

39. Louis Lasagna, "Special Subjects in Human Experimentation," in *Experimentation with Human Subjects*, p. 271.

40. Franz J. Ingelfinger, "Ethics of Experiments on Children," *New England Journal of Medicine* 288 (1973): 791, 792.

41. Charles U. Lowe, Duane Alexander and Barbara Mishkin, "Nontherapeutic Research on Children: An Ethical Dilemma," *The Journal of Pediatrics* 84 (1974): 468–472.

42. *Federal Register* 38 (1973): 31740–31742.

43. William J. Curran and Henry K. Beecher, "Experimentation

in Children: A Reexamination of Legal Ethical Principles," *Journal of the American Medical Association* 210 (1969): 77–83.

44. Ramsey, *The Patient as Person*, pp. 1–58.

45. William E. May, "Experimenting on Human Subjects," *The Linacre Quarterly* 41 (1974): 250.

46. Richard A. McCormick, "Proxy Consent in the Experimentation Situation," in *Love and Society: Essays in the Ethics of Paul Ramsey* ed. James Johnson and David Smith (Missoula, Mont.: Scholars Press, 1974), pp. 221–224.

47. Richard A. McCormick, "Notes on Moral Theology," *Theological Studies* 36 (1975): 127.

48. Curran, *Politics, Medicine and Christian Ethics*, pp. 132–135.

49. McCormick, "Proxy Consent in the Experimentation Situation," in *Love and Society*, p. 218.

50. McCormick's thesis is that one may give proxy consent for another where it is a case of what the other ought to do, but not if it is a work of charity which one could freely choose to do. His explanation of this in terms of the parents' deciding to allow the child to die by not using extraordinary means (ibid., p. 225) seems weak, for ethicians do not usually claim that the child or person ought not to use extraordinary means but can freely choose not to use such means.

51. Paul Ramsey, "The Enforcement of Morals: Nontherapeutic Research on Children," *The Hastings Center Report* 6, no. 4 (August 1976): 21–30; Richard A. McCormick, "Experimentation in Children: Sharing in Sociality," *The Hastings Center Report* 6, no. 6 (December 1976): 41–46; Paul Ramsey, "Children as Research Subjects," *The Hastings Center Report* 7, no. 2 (April 1977): 40–42.

52. *Federal Register* 38 (1973): 31738–31748.

53. See note 7. The eleven-member commission was sworn in on December 3, 1974. The legislation gave the commission a mandate to make recommendations within four months on research involving living fetuses. On July 15, 1975, the commission officially handed in its *Report and Recommendations: Research on the Fetus,* HEW Publication no. (OS) 76–127. There was some disagreement within the commission. The preparation and publication of this report occasioned much discussion about the question of fetal research. See, for example, *Hastings Center Report* 5 no. 3 (June 1975) and no. 5 (October 1975). Subsequent reports have been made by the commission: *Report and Recommendations: Research Involving Prisoners,* October 1, 1976, HEW Publication no. (OS) 76–131; *Report and Recommendations; Psychosurgery,* March 17, 1977, HEW Publication no. (OS) 77–0001; *Report and Recommendations: Disclosure of Research Information Under the Freedom of Information Act,* April 8, 1977, HEW Publication no. (OS) 77–0003. Other reports will be made.

5: Genetics and the Human Future

Through technology and science we human beings have been able to improve our lot in this world. In the last decade science has acquired an almost undreamed-of knowledge about genetics and human genetic development. There is the definite possibility that in the future, and to some extent even now, we can eliminate deleterious genes from the human gene pool and add desirable genes which will improve human individuals and the human species. Thus there arise the ethical problems concerned with interference in our own evolutionary development to better the individual and the human species.

There is another aspect to the problem: we may very well have to interfere in our evolutionary future to prevent a gradual and perhaps even apocalyptic deterioration of the future of the human race. Conditions in modern civilization (e.g., exposure to radiation) bring about deleterious changes in human genetic makeup, while advances in medical science now make it possible for many genetically deficient people to live and reproduce; whereas before modern medicine, such people would die and not be able to reproduce. As a result, there are more and more deleterious genes present in the human gene pool. We may have to intervene to change the human evolutionary process just to avoid possible extinction in the future.

From the outset of the discussion, one must realize that the relationship between the scientist and the ethician is not one of opposition or exclusion. The scientist in her/his own field and in daily life is constantly making ethical decisions. Many conscientious scientists, perhaps influenced by the horrible use of nuclear power, believe they have a duty to make all of us cognizant of the possibilities that lie ahead in the area of human genetics. We should be prepared for such possible developments so that all the people in our society can have a part in determining how the human race will handle the genetic powers that exist now and might exist in the future. All of us humans should be grateful for such attitudes on the part of many scientists. The ethician or moral theologian, on the other hand, does not claim to be a more moral person than any other in society. The ethician tries to study thematically, systematically and reflexively the way in which people make their decisions and to point out those choices believed to be right, good or fitting. (It is difficult to choose a particular word, for different ethical systems would look at it differently.) The Christian ethician looks at a particular problem in the light of the Christian understanding of anthropology and the world. All people are constantly required to make ethical judgments; the professional ethician tries systematically and reflexively to analyze human decisions. Although the ethicist and the scientist have different roles, their functions should be complementary and not antagonistic.

To discuss the problems raised by the possible genetic patterning of human beings, one must first know the scientific facts—the possibilities and the needs. But, unfortunately, many competent scientists disagree on a variety of issues. The theologian can only note such disagreement, since the theologian is incompetent to judge the conflicting opinions. First, the actual situation. Is the genetic future of the human species in danger because of a deleterious gene load in our population? Hermann J. Muller, the late Nobel prize winner, takes a quite pessimistic view: "Thus it is evident that under modern conditions, so long as the dying out is seriously interfered with, human populations must become ever more defective in their genetic constitution, until at long last even the most sophisticated techniques available could no longer suffice to save men from their biological corruptions."[1]

The position advocated by Muller appears to be a minority opinion in the writings on the question. Theodosius Dobzhansky is not as pessimistic about the human future, even though he does admit the problem created by deleterious gene mutations coupled with the fact that modern medicine allows genetically deficient people to live and reproduce. The majority opinion believes that more positive factors, both of a cultural and even of a biological nature, will more than outbalance these negative considerations. "Man is a product of his cultural development as well as of his biological nature. The preponderance of cultural over biological evolution will continue or increase in the foreseeable future."[2] In the meantime, human beings do not have enough knowledge to act in the way envisioned by Muller.

Even if there is no need to intervene in human evolution in the very near future to divert a genetic apocalypse, the ethical problems raised by the fact that we can better the human species still remain. First, it is necessary to briefly summarize the ways in which modern science can now or might be able in the future to control and direct human evolution through genetics.

Although various authors employ diverse terminology, we will speak of three generic types of approach: eugenics, genetic engineering and euphenics.[3]

Eugenics is simply described as good breeding. From a more technical viewpoint, eugenics is described as the selection and recombination of genes already existing in the human gene pool. Negative eugenics aims at removing the deleterious genes from the gene pool. Positive or progressive eugenics tries to improve the genes existing in the gene pool.

The biologists quite generally admit that negative eugenics will have little or no effect in reducing the load of genetic defects in the human species. Recessive genetic defects are generally carried in heterozygotes and thus escape detection. Even if one could detect such recessive genetic defects in heterozygotes, the very fact that most people have some such recessive genetic defects would make it practically impossible to eliminate them from the human population. Negative eugenics is a matter of real concern on a more personal basis in considering problems of the immediate family. Through genetic counselling, a couple may be provided with information which at times should convince them not to marry, or at least not to have children. If a couple knows that the chances are one out of four that their child will be mentally retarded and two out of four that the child will be a carrier of such retardation, there seems to be a strong moral argument not to have children. In addition to voluntary decisions, there could also be laws forbidding such people to marry or also laws requiring the sterilization of some genetically defective people. The compulsory aspect and the interference by the government in the reproductive lives of human beings, however, raise serious moral problems about such solutions in these cases.

Positive eugenics embraces a much more ambitious program for the betterment of the human species. Hermann J. Muller and Julian Huxley think that in the future there may be other means available, but at the present time we must use the means for improving and saving the human species which are already available. Muller proposes that sperm banks be established to store the frozen sperm of men of outstanding characteristics. A panel would decide, preferably after a waiting period of twenty years, which sperm should then be used. Women would then be artificially inseminated with this sperm, and the whole genetic future of the human race would improve. Muller even looks forward to a veritable utopia of never-ending progress in the development of the human species. Although in his later writing he does still occasionally mention such wide-scale utopian schemes and plans, he talks more of the small number who would voluntarily accept such a practice in the beginning. This small group would then serve as an experiment for future development.[4]

A more radical approach, which is not yet possible in the human species, has been suggested by Joshua Lederberg and others. Lederberg speaks of clonal reproduction which, like Muller's suggestion, would begin with the genetic types now known to be strong and make sure these types would be reproduced in great numbers in the future. Clonal reproduction would replicate in an asexual way already existing genotypes. Now science can remove the nucleus from a fertilized frog's egg and replace it with a nucleus from one of the cells of a developing embryo (part of the problem is that the genes must not be already differentiated as is the case in most cells). The fertilized egg thus develops into a frog which is the genetic twin of the frog from which the nucleus of the cell was taken. Cloning would thus be an even surer way than artificial insemination of insuring that genetically gifted people continue to exist and multiply in the future.[5]

A second generic type of approach has been called genetic engineering, genetic surgery, algeny, or transformationist eugenics as distinguished from selectionist eugenics.

The aim of genetic engineering is to change the genes in such a way as to eliminate a certain deleterious type (negative) or to improve the genotype (positive). Genetic engineering aims at changing a particular molecule in the complex structure of the gene. At the present time, science does not have the finesse necessary to change a very specific molecule in the complex structure without affecting other molecules. However, in the future, scientists may be able to direct genetic mutations. Genetic engineering also embraces the phenomena of transformation and transduction. In transformation scientists are now able to take a strain of bacteria not containing a certain genetic property and introduce this property with the DNA extracted from another strain. Transduction tries to transfer such properties through a virus. Such experiments have already been successful with bacteria. However, there are tremendous problems of specificity, directivity and efficiency which must be overcome before genetic engineering could be a possibility on human beings. Also, the fact that human traits have a polygenic base greatly complicates the problem. The individual diversity of every human being tends to make some scientists quite pessimistic about the future possibilities of genetic engineering. Others, however, think it remains a real possibility even though it might be many years away.

A third generic type of improving the human species has been called euphenics. Euphenics is somewhere between eugenics and euthenics or environmental engineering. In the past, and probably even more so in the future, human development occurs primarily because of our intervention in and control over our environment. Lederberg has proposed euphenics as that part of euthenics concerned with human environment. Euphenics aims at the control and regulation of the phenotype rather than the genotype. This would involve all efforts at controlling gene expression in human beings without changing the genotype and thus would not involve hereditary changes. Eye glasses to correct poor vision is one example; insulin for diabetes sufferers is another. Lederberg believes there are a number of areas in which medical science should proceed: accelerated engineering in the development of artificial organs; development of industrial methodology for synthesis of specific proteins; eugenic experiments with animals to produce genetically homogeneous materials for spare parts in humans. Lederberg was arguing in 1962 that priority should now be given to euphenics and then later to long-range eugenic concerns of the human genotype.[6] Also, there is the future possibility that science will know how to switch on and off different genes at specific periods of development and greatly change the individual.

In general, these are the various ways in which it might be scientifically possible to interfere in and direct our own development. At the present time, the only available positive means which might be efficacious are the positive eugenics proposed by Muller. Many scientists would agree with Paul Ramsey, the Christian ethicist from Princeton, that the means that are now possible raise more moral problems than the forms of genetic engineering possible in the future.[7] Many scientists, in fact the majority writing on the subject, are also unwilling at the present time to accept the proposals of Muller on both scientific and moral grounds. The majority of scientists are raising these questions today primarily for discussion so that in the future the human race is not suddenly confronted with these problems without having thought of any way to cope with them.[8] This study too will follow that general approach and consider primarily the various elements in the discussion which raise problems not only about the ethical use of this scientific power, but also raise methodological questions for moral theology itself. First, the area of moral theology.

I. Moral Theology

At first it might seem strange that possible advances in human control over heredity should raise problems for moral theology itself. History, however, reminds us of the dangers of a totally *a priori* theological approach to newer developments in science. Theology is not totally settled once and for all, but itself is in a continual process of growth and change. Moral theology as the study of Christians and their actions is constantly in dialogue with the empirical and social sciences to try to understand better human beings and human actions. This section will develop three dangers that a theological methodology must avoid, or more positively, three emphases that must be present in any theological approach to the problems raised by our possible power over our own future development.

The first emphasis that must be present in the approach of moral theology is a greater appreciation of historicity and historical consciousness. Catholic theology, in many ways following the lead of Protestant theology, first adopted an historical perspective through the renewal of the study of Scripture. The Scriptures as the Word of God in the words of humans are historically and culturally limited documents. Theology has also learned from the mistakes of the liberal Protestant movement in the nineteenth and twentieth centuries in assuming an overly simple identity between the historical experience of the contemporary interpreter and the first century biblical witness.[9]

The notion of historicity or historical development has been employed by some theologians to show that the teachings of Gregory XVI and Pius IX in the area of religious liberty were not contradicted by the later teachings of Vatican II. In the light of the historical contexts of the times, both teachings could be correct in their own circumstances.[10] John Courtney Murray saw the primary reason for the different approaches to religious liberty in the different understanding of the role and function of the state in the nineteenth and twentieth centuries. Perhaps those theologians who have been defending the teaching of the nineteenth century popes on religious liberty have been somewhat too indulgent in explaining the total difference in terms of historicity.[11] But at least Catholic theology is realizing the need for an historical understanding in its approach.

The growth and progress of modern civilization in all areas, not only in science and technology, have made contemporary theology more aware of historical growth and change. Changes in politics, science, economics and sociology cannot remain unreflected in approaches to moral theology. Philosophy today illustrates the greater emphasis on historicity in many of its contemporary trends such as process philosophy. According to Rahner, theology's possibility of error is ultimately rooted in its historical character.[12] The very fact that contemporary advances in the science of genetics raise problems and dangers for moral theology is another indication of the historicity of theology itself.

A more historically conscious theology will tend to have a different concept of anthropology—a concept that is more open than closed. Human beings are not totally determined by a fixed nature existing within the self. The genius of modern man and woman is the ability toward self-creation and self-direction. We are constantly open to a tremendous variety of actions and options. Any theological position based on a closed concept of human nature as being something already within the self to which the individual must conform oneself and one's actions will be an inaccurate understanding of the human reality and tend to result in unacceptable moral conclusions. Thus the predominant concept can no longer be an immutable and unchangeable nature, but rather the concept of historicity. Notice that historicity provides both for continuity and discontinuity, thus avoiding the extremes of an immobile classicism or the complete discontinuity of sheer existentialism.

In the area of questions raised by the possible drastic developments in genetics, the theologian must be ever mindful of the need for an historical approach, but must also avoid the danger of uncritically accepting every new scientific possibility as being something necessarily human and good.

The progressive eugenics proposed by Muller would call for the separation of procreation and the love union aspect of sexuality. Christian ethics has generally maintained that these two aspects are joined by the design of the Creator and Redeemer, and human beings cannot separate what God has joined together. However, there is a methodological problem in proving such a fact by merely citing the first chapters of Genesis in which the unitive and procreative nature of human sexuality is taught. Obviously, the teaching of Genesis is quite historically conditioned. Can the theologian merely extrapolate from the circumstances of Genesis and make an absolute and universal norm for the understanding of human sexuality? There are definite dangers in that approach.

Paul Ramsey argues against the plan proposed by Muller precisely because it breaks the bond between the procreative and the love union aspects of sexuality. Ramsey, however, does not base his argument primarily on Genesis, or creation, or nature. Ramsey argues primarily from the "Second Article of the Creed" as specifying the Christian concept of creation and conjugal love in the Prologue of John's Gospel and the fifth chapter of the Letter to the Ephesians. Just as the creative and redeeming act of God is a life-giving act of love, so human sexuality is both procreative and loving. Ephesians 5 contains the ultimate reference for the meaning and nature of conjugal love.[13] It seems, nevertheless, that the teaching which Ramsey finds in Ephesians 5 might also be historically conditioned.

I do believe that at the present time in our circumstances sexuality has its proper expression, value and meaning in the marital realm within which the procreative and love union aspects of sexuality are joined together. However, one can envision a possibility in which greater values might be at stake and call for some type of altering the way in which Christian marriage now tries to preserve these important values. For example, if the dire predictions of Muller were universally accepted and the human race did face a genetic apocalypse in the near future, then the entire situation might be changed. It seems that even the Scriptures witness many cases in which the understanding of marriage had to be changed because of the conditions of the times (e.g., polygamy). Ramsey himself does admit some possible relativity in his teaching by saying that there might be some redeeming features in Muller's proposals, but this is not "sufficient to place the practice in the class of morally permitted actions."[14] I agree with Ramsey's understanding of things as they are at present, but his argumentation and his prospects in the future do not seem to give enough place to historicity. However, for an individual sterile couple AID in my judgment even now cannot be morally excluded in all cases even though AID might entail some problems.

A second danger in the approach of moral theology to genetics is the danger of an individualistic methodology and the failure to emphasize the communitarian and societal dimensions of reality. Christian thinking deserves much credit for upholding the dignity of the individual which in many ways is also the foundation of our modern society, although at times Christian practice has not always lived up to Christian theory. Today, however, we human beings are much more conscious of our communitarian nature and our relationships with all other people and the world. The approach of moral theology will have to balance more adroitly the proper claims of the individual with the claims of society. The Christian notions of *agape, koinonia,* and the reign of God all seem to be more open to communitarian and social understandings. Problems facing contemporary society in politics, sociology and economics all show a greater role being given to the communitarian, the social and the cosmic. Moral theology cannot employ models that are exclusively individualistic or narrowly interpersonal.[15]

In the past, moral theology has been somewhat ambivalent about the tension between the individual and the community. In many areas the approach has been too individualistic; whereas there were other instances in which too much stress was placed on the power of the community over the rights of the individual. For example, theologians affirmed the obligation of the defendant to publicly admit his guilt which denied the right of the individual not to incriminate oneself by admitting one's own guilt.[16] Also, the failure to accept religious liberty shows an unwillingness to accept the total freedom and dignity of the individual.

The area of social ethics furnishes an example where Catholic theology was too individualistic in its approach. Perhaps such an emphasis can be explained in the light of a reaction to communism and socialism. Lately some Catholics have become upset at the papal call for socialization which they look upon as an invasion of the rights of the individual. Pope John, in his social encyclicals, emphasized the social aspect while still preserving the legitimate claims of the individual by basing his social ethics on the two principles of subsidiarity and socialization. These two principles try to keep in tension the legitimate demands of the individual and society.[17] The same danger of individualism can be seen in the overemphasis on private property in some Catholic teaching. The social teaching of Leo XIII acknowledged the social aspect of property, but it was not emphasized. Today, Catholic theology is stressing the social aspect of property because the goods of creation exist primarily for all human beings. *Populorum Progressio* of Paul VI well illustrates the more communal and social emphasis required today.[18]

Too individualistic a concept of anthropology has also affected Catholic understandings of medical morality, especially as this was influenced by the principle of totality. Pope Pius XII developed the principle of totality in many of his discourses on medical matters. According to the principle of totality, the individual may dispose of the members or functions of one's body for the good of the whole, but a part may be sacrificed "only when there is the subordination of part to whole that exists in the natural body."[19] Pius XII wrote in the context of totalitarian governments, and was very careful to deny that by virtue of the principle of totality the government had power over the life of the individual, for the individual is not merely a part of the totality which is the state. At times, Pius XII limited the application of totality to physical organisms with their physical unity or totality.[20] Thus the principle of totality cannot be used to justify the transplantation of organs or experimentation for the good of others, since in this case the strict relationship of part to physical whole does not exist. Some Catholic theologians went further and denied that organic transplantation or experimentation for the good of others was morally permitted.[21] Other theologians justified such practices, however, either by introducing other principles (e.g., charity) or by attempting to expand the principle of totality itself.[22] Thus the principle of totality, at least in its narrower understanding and application, apart from other considerations, can overly emphasize the individual at the expense of other aspects of reality.

The present historical situation calls for a greater understanding of human beings as existing in community with each other, intertwined with many different relationships. The task for moral theology as also mentioned in chapter four, is to develop a methodology which does justice to the communitarian, s :ial and cosmic needs of the present without falling into a collectivism. The ever growing consciousness of the one world in which we all share has tended to underline the need for a more communitarian approach. The economic problems of England and the United States affect the whole world; the fashions of Paris become available all over the world; the political decisions in Moscow, Peking and Washington have repercussions around the world. Science through its many steps in controlling our environment has affected many people.

Precisely in the area of genetics and heredity the individual realizes the existence of other responsibilities which limit one's own options and freedom. Traditional Catholic theology has recognized some limitations in this area. The older manuals of theology spoke of the primary end of marriage which included the procreation and education of offspring. Responsible parenthood is a moral imperative for couples, and responsible parenthood entails some responsibility for the children who will be born and to the race itself.[23] Genetic reasons at times should compel a couple not to marry or not to bring children into the world. If offspring have a one out of four chance of being severely retarded and a two out of four chance of becoming carriers of severe retardation, it seems the couple have a moral obligation to refrain from having children.

What about the possibility that the community might positively intervene to prevent and prohibit such marriages? In the past, Catholic theology has been willing to accept some limitations on marriage. The impediments to marriage in the Code of Canon Law include consanguinity, which may even have been based on some eugenic reasoning. Another question arises about the compulsory sterilization of certain classes of people. I believe that this interference with the individual person is not called for today, especially without a first attempt to employ genetic counseling on a wide scale. Most scientists writing in this area are also somewhat unwilling to propose such compulsory measures. There also looms in the minds of many the abuses of power to which such practices would be susceptible. Chapter seven discusses these questions in greater detail.

The very complexity of the problem will in the long run call for some community control. In other areas of human life the more power that an individual has and the more complex things become, the greater is the need for community intervention and control. Things from the right of people to fly their own airplanes to the rights of people to hunt and fish, to say nothing of the daily questions in the order of economics, politics and education, have required some type of community control. The very power which science and genetics can bring into existence must be under some greater control than the individual can provide. In the not-too-distant future, there may well be need for some type of community control in the area of genetics and heredity. What if science acquires the power to determine the sex of children? Tremendous problems could very easily result for society if the proportion between the sexes was greatly affected. This would have ramifications in just about every other sector of human existence. The stability of families and the basic social structure of our society would be somewhat threatened. Society could not allow an unbalanced proportion of the sexes to exist for a long time. What could be done? Society could forbid its members to use such means of determining the sex of their children, or it could set up an elaborate system of control. Obviously there will be many problems no matter which choice is made. The point is that society may very well have to make such a choice. Nor can one avoid the problem by merely condemning the research that might lead to such power. I am not euphoric at the prospect of controlling such power, but such power presents us with the creative challenge to use it for human betterment despite all the inherent human limitations.

My contention is that the complexity and inter-relatedness of human existence, plus the tremendous power that science may put into human hands, are going to call for a more communitarian and social approach to the moral decisions facing our society.

A third required emphasis in the approach of moral theology to questions raised by our control over our own hereditary future concerns the dominion and the power which one has over one's own life. Christian thought has constantly emphasized that the individual does not have complete dominion over one's own life. The human creature is the steward of the gift of life received from the Creator; final human destiny lies outside and beyond this world. On the other hand, the human being is the glory of creation and the greatest sign of God's handiwork in this world.

Today more than ever in the past the human person is conscious of the power that one has over one's life and future. Catholic theologians do not hesitate to say that the human being is a self-creator, for in a sense the individual is unfinished and capable now of creating oneself. The power of self-creation has always been rooted in the spiritual power of oneself—a truth recognized by Thomas Aquinas. Aquinas does not hesitate to see "man as an image of God" precisely because he is "endowed with intelligence, free will, and a power of his actions which is proper to him . . . having dominion over his own activities."[24] Thanks to the marvels of science, the rational creature is now able to extend this dominion into many other facets of existence.

The Christian attitude toward anthropology tries to balance or even hold in dialectical tension two aspects—human greatness precisely because one is free and guide of one's own development on the one hand, and human creatureliness and sinfulness on the other hand. Corresponding to these two aspects of human existence are what the older theological tradition has called the two capital sins of sloth and pride. Harvey Cox has pointed out that too frequently we forget that the great sin is sloth or the failure to take responsibility for the world which is ours to make.[25] Although at times sloth has been an often neglected aspect of Christian life, Cox and others should not forget the terrible evils connected with pride through which human beings have used all kinds of power—social, economic, political, military and even religious—to pursue their own particular ends and gain advantage over others.[26] The proper Christian approach must be cognizant of both these aspects in the use and abuse of the power and dominion which belongs to human beings. Just as Cox has at times overemphasized sloth and neglected pride, Paul Ramsey, especially in his writing on genetics, seems to overemphasize *hubris* or pride. "In fact it may be said that the ethical violations we have noted on the *horizontal plane* (coercive breeding or nonbreeding, injustice done to individuals or to mishaps, the violation of the nature of human parenthood) are a function of a more fundamental happening in the *vertical* dimension, namely *hubris,* and playing God."[27] Certainly Ramsey is correct in seeing that some genetic proposals do fail to take account of human limitations and sinfulness; but one cannot deny that since human beings have a greater dominion over their lives and futures today, there is the danger of not using responsibly the dominion or power they either have now or may possess in the future.

Although I agree with most of Ramsey's conclusions on the questions of genetics at the present time, I believe he does not give enough importance to the aspects of historicity and the greater dominion which human beings have today. Both of these differences stem from a basic theological stance because of which I would attribute greater importance to efforts in cooperating with the building of the new heaven and the new earth. This difference raises the fundamental problem for the Christian ethicist of ethics and eschatology. Ramsey views eschatology primarily, and sometimes exclusively, in terms of apocalypse: "Religious people have never denied, indeed they affirm, that God means to kill us all in the end, and in the end He is going to succeed. Anyone who intends the world as a Jew or as a Christian—to the measure in which this is his mode of being in the world—goes forth to meet the collision of planets or the running down of suns, and he exists toward a future that may contain a genetic Apocalypse with his eyes fixed on another *eschaton*...."[28] Ramsey rightly emphasizes the aspect of apocalypse or discontinuity between this world and the next against the naive progressivists who see the future age in perfect continuity with the present. However, it seems that Christian eschatology includes three aspects, all of which have to be retained if one is going to have a proper understanding of the relationship between this world and the next: the teleological, the apocalyptic and the prophetic.[29]

By stressing just the apocalyptic, Ramsey fails to give the due but limited importance to human efforts in cooperating with God in bringing about the new heaven and the new earth. Although Ramsey may emphasize exclusively the apocalyptic aspect of eschatology because of his polemic against the humanistic, progressive mentality which sees us as bringing about the blessed future through our own efforts and technology, nevertheless, his entire ethical theory seems to rest on an eschatology which overly stresses the apocalyptic. Precisely because of such an eschatology, Ramsey sees Christian ethics based on the model of deontological ethics rather than the model of teleology or responsibility.[30]

Human beings do have more dominion over life today than in the past—a fact that has already had a great impact on Catholic moral theology. The dissatisfaction with some explanations of natural law theory, especially as illustrated by arguments against artificial contraception, stems from the fact that we now have the power and ability to interfere with the physical and biological laws of nature. Scientific and technological progress have given us a greater power over both life and death so that today Catholic theologians even acknowledge "the right to die."[31] All these indications point out the need for theologians to be very precise and cautious in applying the notion of limited human dominion over life to the theological questions raised by advances in genetics. The contemporary Christian does have greater dominion and control over life, although the creature will never have complete dominion over one's life and future.

II. Genetic Proposals

This study will criticize from a viewpoint of Catholic moral theology some of the attitudes seen in various approaches of scientists. Especially in the proposals of Muller, there is a utopian outlook on the future; although in his later writings, Muller appeared to be somewhat less utopian than in his earlier writings. His proposals were scaled down somewhat to an experimental nucleus, but his overall goal remained. "By these means the way can be opened up for unlimited progress in the genetic constitution of man to match and reinforce his cultural progress, and reciprocally to be reinforced by it, in a perhaps never-ending succession."[32] Muller advocates the use of sperm banks and artificial insemination of women with this superior semen because there are no other means available at present. He does not think other techniques of genetic surgery will be available until the twenty-first century, if then; but such genetic surgery may very well "do much better than nature has done."[33]

Muller does recognize an element of the tragic in the human, but he believes many of the problems could be overcome by progressive eugenics. "Thus, men grievously need the Golden Rule, but the Golden Rule grievously needs men in whose very nature it is more deeply rooted than in ours. These men would not require the wills of saints, for their way of life would be normal to them. They would take it for granted, and could live full wholesome lives, joyously carrying out the ever greater enterprises made possible for their strengthened individual initiative, working hand in hand in free alliance with their enhanced cooperative functionings. At the same time their personal relationships would be warmer and more genuine, so that they could enjoy more of the love that gives itself away. Along with this, less forcing would be required of them in extending their feelings of kinship to those more remote from their contacts."[34]

The Christian vision of human existence cannot accept any utopian schemes. Modern life and science do give us much greater dominion than we had before, but each remains a creature and a sinner. The final stage of the reign of God is in the future and not totally continuous with our present existence. Although in the past, many Christians may have been guilty of what has been called "eschatological irresponsibility," since they forgot about the possibility of bringing about a relative justice here and now, contemporary Christians can never forget the transcendent aspect of the reign of God which is his gracious gift to us. Science and technology can do much to help, but they cannot overcome the creatureliness and sinfulness which mark human existence in the Christian perspective.

Christian theology has also learned from its own history the dangers of utopian thinking and the temptations of a naively optimistic outlook on human growth and progress. Some Roman Catholics naively looked to the past and saw a romantic utopia in the thirteenth, the greatest of centuries. Liberal Protestantism less than a century ago made the mistake of thinking that we could bring about the kingdom of God in this world by our own work and effort. Christian theologians are chastened by the remark (in my judgment too negative and critical) of H. Richard Niebuhr about such attempts to bring about the reign of God in this world. "In this one-sided view of progress which saw the growth of the wheat, but not that of the tares, the gathering of the grain, but not the burning of the chaff, this liberalism was indeed naively optimistic. A God without wrath brought men without sin into a kingdom without judgment through the ministrations of a Christ without a cross."[35] Christians should realize the important contributions that science can make, but the Christian knows only one Lord and Messiah—Christ Jesus. Biology or genetics will never completely overcome inherent human limitations and sinfulness.

The ambitious genetic proposals of Muller (sperm banks) and Lederberg (cloning) would call for large-scale changes in our contemporary society if they are to be successful even from a biological viewpoint. Lederberg points out that a system of tempered clonality would be necessary to provide for the variety and adaptability necessary if the human gene pool is to progress. Thus some people would reproduce clonally and some sexually.[36] Among the many problems that would arise for both Muller and Lederberg would be the selection of the ideal types. Who is to decide? What criteria are to be employed? How do we know if a person will do as well in a different type of environment? Why is it that many children of geniuses have not made great contributions themselves? Even Muller agrees that we would have a difficult time selecting the ideal person and what characteristics such a person should have. Commentators occasionally note that Muller himself changed his opinion about who would be ideal types. In 1935 he claimed no woman would refuse to have a child by Lenin, but a later list leaves Lenin out of the acceptable "fathers."[37] All these problems are raised to illustrate the complexities that are often not given sufficient attention by the proponents of such approaches.

Human history seems to confirm the Christian understanding of human limitation and sinfulness. Even if human beings do acquire such tremendous power over genetics and heredity, there is every indication that such power will not always be used for the good of humanity. History shows that humans use power for evil as well as for good: the horrible use of eugenics by totalitarian regimes still is a clear and horrendous memory in the minds of many people. Industrialization has brought about a tremendous increase in economic power, but such power probably has been used more often to exploit rather than to help poor people and poor nations. Scientists themselves frequently have pangs of conscience over the uses made of nuclear power. Even the seemingly neutral accomplishments of technology reveal the ambiguity concomitant in human existence. The automobile has brought with it many contributions to a more human life; but it has also brought with it staggering accidental death tolls, air pollution, the disruption of poor people from their homes and the spoiling of natural beauty. A good number of people in our country today, to say nothing of the total world, are dissatisfied with both the foreign and domestic policies of the government. Have dominance and self-interest not played the greatest roles in the shaping of our foreign policy? Does the priority of certain domestic programs indicate a true willingness to share the goods of our society with others or rather an attempt to make sure that the gulf widens between the "haves" and the "have nots" in society? The very thought that our genetic planners would be of the same type as our domestic, economic, political, and foreign policy planners does not augur for a utopia on the way.

Catholic theologians generally admit the axiom that abuse does not take away the use. Preliminary discussion and planning might help to eliminate some possible abuses, but some will always remain. History again indicates that as more solutions are found, further questions and problems will also arise. Utopia will always be outside the reach of the creature. It is important to note that the vast majority of the scientists writing on this issue disavow the utopian proposals put forth, for example, by Muller. Also in fairness to Lederberg, he has not to my knowledge advocated the proposal of clonal reproduction although he does mention it as a very likely possibility, if and when it is biologically possible. Lederberg and others believe it is their obligation to inform the general public about the problems all of us might be facing in the not too distant future.

A second danger found in the writings of some scientists is the identification of the scientific with the human, but the human includes much more than just science and technology. *A fortiori* a Christian anthropology embraces more than the limited horizon of science and technology, for the scientific approach to a particular question is only a partial aspect of the whole reality. The scientific and the human do not necessarily coincide, thus there exists a potential source of conflict. This danger was pointed out by Pope Pius XII in an address to the First International Symposium on Genetics in 1953.[38] The very fact that we are scientifically capable of doing something does not mean that it should be done, for we must control the evolution and development of science. Too often one has the impression that it is science and technology that are going to control human existence. People today are somewhat aware of the need to give human direction and guidance to technology. Just because our nation has the ability and knowledge to send a man to the moon does not mean that such projects should have priority over more pressing human needs. Just because science can keep a dying person alive for a few more hours, does not mean that such means should be employed. At times there are important human values involved which should not be sacrificed for the good of any science.

Such a narrowness of view does seem to color some of the writings of Muller. Muller argues that we should use the means now available, a progressive eugenic program through sperm banks and AID, rather than wait for the genetic surgery which might be available in the next century. His argumentation is most revealing. "The obstacles to carrying out such an improvement by selection are psychological ones, based on antiquated traditions from which we can emancipate ourselves, but the obstacles to do so by treatment of the genetic materials are substantive ones rooted in the inherent difficulties of the physico-chemical situation."[39] Notice that the only substantive obstacles are those rooted in the biological order.

Muller dismisses the obstacles in the way of his progressive eugenics program as merely "psychological ones based on antiquated traditions." Thus there seem to be no obstacles that stand in the way of scientific development and scientific goals other than those things to which science has not as yet found a suitable answer. However, it does seem there can be and there are important human values which would stand in the way of the geneticist on some occasions. I am sure that not even Muller would allow the scientist to experiment on human beings the same way in which one experiments on bacteria. Elsewhere Muller refers to the primary obstacle standing in the way of the adoption of his eugenic program as the attitude of "individual, genetic proprietorship, or pride of so-called blood."[40] But many people see in these obstacles very important human and moral values, since parenthood and family bonds are more than antiquated traditions. For the Christian, the bond between procreation and love union is more than a mere arbitrary arrangement even if one can envision certain historical situations in which it might be sacrificed for greater values.

The narrowness of vision of one who sees all reality through the eyes of an individual science can be illustrated by the consequences that such a program might have on many other facets of human existence. A sociologist, for example, would have some very significant aspects to add to the total human picture. Marriage and family serve important functions and roles in our contemporary society. If sexual behavior is separated from reproduction, why should there be any regulation of sexual behavior at all? Muller's plan would raise grave problems for the psychologist who would then have to try to find some substitute for the stability and deep personal relationships which are now provided for in marriage and the family. For the ethician all these things also constitute important moral values. To the extent that a scientist fails to see all these other aspects or dismisses them as antiquated traditions, the scientist shows the narrowness and the ultimate "a-humanness" of a narrowly scientific vision.

The third danger follows from what has been said about the difference between the scientific horizon and the ultimate human horizon. The scientific and technical worlds view reality primarily in terms of effects and performances; they are success oriented and thus totally interested in results and effects. Thus there arise several sources of conflict with the human and the Christian horizon. The first potential area of difference concerns the ultimate reason for the dignity of the human person which, from the Christian perspective, cannot be measured in terms of utility or performance. The greatness of human life stems from the free gift of the loving God of creation. The Christian notion of love modeled on the love of Yahweh for his people and Christ for his Church indicates that the ultimate reason for the lovability of a person does not depend on one's qualities or deeds or successes or failures; in fact, the covenant commitment of God to his chosen people appears as a sheer gift, especially in the light of the constant infidelities of his people. Christian anthropology does not see human value primarily in terms of what one does or can do for self or others, but in terms of what God has first done for the creature.

On the level of ethical theory, an overemphasis on the importance of effects leads to a theory of consequentialism. There is the danger of seeing all moral values in terms of consequences so that the model of the means-end relationship becomes centrally normative. Our basic human intuitions reject the manipulative spirit that tries to use everything as a means for a further end; e.g., we react against people "using friends" or "using other human lives," etc. Thus, especially in the area of genetics, Ramsey has pointed out the need for an ethic of means as well as an ethic of ends, since there are certain values that cannot be sacrificed as means for certain other ends.[41] Pius XII, in his 1953 address, likewise pointed out the danger of making a good end justify any means.[42] However, in Catholic moral theology there has been a tendency to view the means-end relationship in too physical a manner and to forget that on occasion the end truly specifies the means.[43]

Most scientists are aware of the possible collision of values and other problems arising from the difference between the human and the scientific horizons. Some scientists, for example, see no problem in performing certain experiments on plants or animals, but they would not do such experimentation on humans. Lederberg himself has brought up the problem of the first experiment in genetic surgery and especially the first attempts to clone a human being.[44] One cannot experiment on human beings in the same way that one experiments on bacteria. This problem of experimentation will become even more acute in the future. This problem will be faced long before the problems created by the use of new techniques for directing the human evolutionary process.

The same problem has another face. The scientists I have read readily admit human dignity, and they constantly emphasize that nothing should be done to a person without consent. This respect for human dignity is admirable. Again, however, I would agree with Ramsey in pointing out that one is the body of one's soul just as much as one is the soul of one's body.[45] In more modern terms, we are not merely our freedom but also our corporality. One can offend against a person not only by violating one's spirituality, but also one's corporality. There is the danger of a neodualism that sees the human being only as spirit. The very fact that a person consents to something does not mean that the act is thus necessarily right. Such a principle is rejected in our jurisprudence which holds that a person cannot give up inalienable rights even by consent. Too often today in many ethical problems one hears the saying that there is nothing wrong with it provided that everybody agrees and consents. Unfortunately, the Catholic tradition has tended to make the biological normative, but the opposite extreme of paying no attention to corporality also goes against human dignity precisely insofar as it is human. The ecological crisis should make us more aware of our corporality.

This study has tried to raise some of the dangers both from the viewpoint of theology and the viewpoint of biology which will be present in the future discussions about the control of human evolution. Since the scientists themselves and especially Ramsey have given extensive ethical criticisms of some of the genetic proposals, this paper concentrated more on the problems such genetic questions raise for moral theology or Christian ethics. I agree with most scientists that now is the time to begin discussing these important issues. In the meantime, it seems that voluntary negative eugenics should be encouraged through a more widespread use of genetic counseling. The majority of the scientists themselves who have written in this area do not believe that the program proposed by Muller should be put into practice even from the limited viewpoint of biology. From the moral viewpoint, I agree that such a program should not be adopted now. In my view, whatever the future brings, it will not be a utopia. Scientific advances will also bring problems and difficulties especially in the control of such great power that we will have. However, these problems are not sufficient reason to stop all experimentation and work toward acquiring a greater power over human heredity and genes. In the experimentation and continual probing, it will be necessary to respect human dignity and not totally subordinate the individual to the goals of scientific advancement. Since we may have much greater power within this century, it is not too early to continue in a more structured way the dialogue which has already been initiated.

NOTES

1. Hermann J. Muller, "Better Genes for Tomorrow," in *The Population Crisis and the Use of World Resources,* ed. Stuart Mudd (The Hague: Dr. W. Junk Publishers, 1964), p. 315. For most of Muller's articles and addresses in the field of genetics before 1961, see *Studies in Genetics: The Selected Papers of H. J. Muller* (Bloomington, Ind.: Indiana University Press, 1962).

2. Theodosius Dobzhansky, "Changing Man," *Science* 155 (1967): 409. Dobzhansky (p. 411) maintains that we do not have enough knowledge to be sure of the value, even from the biological perspective, of humankind freed from all genetic loads. For a fuller explanation of his thought, see Dobzhansky, *Mankind Evolving* (New Haven:

Yale University Press, 1962). Others who also are not as pessimistic as Muller and maintain the need to wait for more knowledge include: S. E. Lurie, "Directed Genetic Change: Perspectives from Molecular Genetics," in *The Control of Human Heredity and Evolution*, ed. T. M. Sonneborn (New York: Macmillan, 1965); John Maynard Smith, "Eugenics and Utopia," *Daedalus* 94 (1965): 487–505; Curt Stern, "Genes and People," *Perspectives in Biology and Medicine* 10 (1966–67): 500–523; and many others.

3. In the preparation of this study, in addition to the bibliography already mentioned, the following studies from the scientific viewpoint were helpful: E. Shils, et al., *Life or Death: Ethics and Options* (Seattle: University of Washington Press, 1968); Frederick Osborne, *The Future of Human Heredity* (New York: Weybright and Talley, 1968); John D. Roslansky, ed., *Genetics and the Future of Man* (New York: Appleton-Century-Crofts, 1966); T. M. Sonneborn, ed., *The Control of Human Heredity and Evolution* (New York: Macmillan, 1965); Gordon Wolstenholme, ed., *Man and His Future* (Boston: Little, Brown, and Co., 1963). Also, Leonard Ornstein, "The Population Explosion, Conservative Eugenics, and Human Evolution," *Bulletin of the Atomic Scientists* 23 (June 1967): 57–60; Joshua Lederberg, "Experimental Genetics and Human Evolution," *Bulletin of the Atomic Scientists* 22 (Oct. 1966): 4–11; James F. Crowe "The Quality of People: Human Evolutionary Changes," *Bioscience* 16 (1966): 863–867; N. H. Horowitz, "Perspectives in Medical Genetics," *Perspectives in Biology and Medicine* 9 (1965/66): 349–357; Roland D. Hotchkiss, "Portents for a Genetic Engineering," *Journal of Heredity* 56 (1965):197–202; T. M. Sonneborn, "Genetics and Man's Vision," *Proceedings of the American Philosophical Society* 109 (August 1965): 237–241; Sonneborn, "Implications of the New Genetics for Biology and Man," *A.I.B.S. Bulletin* 13 (April 1963): 22–26. (A.I.B.S. is the American Institute of Biological Sciences).

4. Later articles by Muller include: "Genetic Progress by Voluntarily Conducted Germinal Choice," *Man and His Future*, pp. 247–262: "Means and Aims in Human Genetic Betterment," *The Control of Human Heredity and Evolution*, pp. 100–123. Julian Huxley, *The Humanist Frame* (London: Allen and Unwin, 1961); *Eugenics in Evolutionary Perspective* (London: Eugenics Society, 1962); *Essays of a Humanist* (New York: Harper and Row, 1964).

5. Lederberg, *Bulletin of the Atomic Scientists* 22 (October 1966): 4–11.

6. Joshua Lederberg, "Biological Future of Man," in *Man and His Future*, pp. 263–273.

7. Paul Ramsey, "Moral and Religious Implications in Genetic Control," in *Genetics and the Future of Man*, p. 153.

8. This conclusion is based on the works cited above and is the

same conclusion reached by James M. Gustafson in reviewing *Life or Death: Ethics and Options* in *Commonweal* 89 (4 Oct. 1968): 28.

9. Lloyd J. Averill, *American Theology in the Liberal Tradition* (Philadelphia: Westminster Press, 1967), pp. 125–127.

10. Roger Aubert, "La liberté religieuse du Syllabus de 1864 á nos jours," *Recherches et Débats* 50 (1965): 13–25. Among Murray's many writings, see especially for this aspect, John Courtney Murray, S.J. *The Problem of Religious Freedom* (Westminster, Md.: Newman Press 1965).

11. Etienne Borne, "Le problème majeur du Syllabus: vérité et liberté," *Recherches et Débats* 50 (1965): 26–42.

12. Karl Rahner, S. J., "The Historical Dimension in Theology," *Theology Digest*, Sesquicentennial Issue (1968): 30–42.

13. Ramsey, *Genetics and the Future of Man*, pp. 145–147.

14. Ibid., p. 159.

15. Johannes B. Metz, "Relationship of Church and World in the Light of a Political Theology," *Theology of Renewal* II, ed. L. K. Shook, C. S. B. (New York: Herder and Herder, 1968), pp. 255–270; Metz, "The Church's Social Function in the Light of a Political Theology," *Concilium* 36 (June 1968): 2–18.

16. Patrick Granfield, O. S. B., "The Right to Silence," *Theological Studies* 26 (1965): 280–298; 27 (1966): 401–420.

17. John F. Cronin, S. S., *The Social Teaching of Pope John XXIII* (Milwaukee: Bruce Publishing Co., 1963).

18. For a fine summary of this changing emphasis, see Edward Duff, S. J., "Property, Private," *New Catholic Encyclopedia* 11: 849–855.

19. Gerald Kelly, S. J., *Medico-Moral Problems* (St. Louis: Catholic Hospital Association, 1958), p. 247.

20. *Acta Apostolicae Sedis* 44 (1952): 786; 48 (1956): 461 (hereafter referred to as *A.A.S.*).

21. Gerald Kelly, S. J., "Pope Pius XII and the Principle of Totality," *Theological Studies* 16 (1955): 373–396. A summary and applications of the principle of totality are found in Kelly, *Medico-Moral Problems*, pp. 8–11; 245–269. Kelly on the basis of other moral principles would allow organic transplants and experimentation for the good of others. Note that Kelly wrote before the address of Pius XII in 1958 in which Pius developed and extended the principle of totality: "To the subordination, however, of the particular organs to the organism and its own finality, one must add the subordination of the organism to the spiritual finality of the person himself." *A.A.S.* 50 (1958): 693, 694.

22. For an interpretation which broadens the notion of totality in the light of Pius' 1958 discourse, see Martin Nolan, O. S. A., *The*

Principle of Totality in the Writings of Pope Pius XII (Rome: Pontifical Gregorian University, 1960).
  23. Bernard Häring, *Marriage in the Modern World* (Westminster, Md.: Newman Press, 1966), pp. 312–323.
  24. *Summa Theologiae, I*II*ᵃᵉ*, Prologue.
  25. Harvey G. Cox, *On Not Leaving It to the Snake* (New York: Macmillan, 1967), "Introduction: Faith and Decision" and throughout the book.
  26. E.g., Reinhold Niebuhr, *Moral Man and Immoral Society* (New York: Charles Scribner's Sons, 1933 and 1960); *Love and Justice: Selections from the Shorter Writings of Reinhold Niebuhr*, ed. D. B. Robertson (Cleveland: Meridian Books, 1967), especially pp. 46–54.
  27. Paul Ramsey, "Shall We Clone a Man?" in *Who Shall Live:*, ed. Kenneth Vaux (Philadelphia: Fortress Press, 1970). This problem of the greater dominion possessed by modern human beings who still remain sinful creatures is recognized by Leroy Augenstein, *Come, Let Us Play God* (New York: Harper and Row, 1969).
  28. Ramsey, *Genetics and the Future of Man*, p. 136.
  29. Harvey Cox, "Evolutionary Progress and Christian Promise," *Concilium* 26 (June 1967): 35–47; M. C. Vanhengal, O. P., and J. Peters, "Death and Afterlife," *Concilium* 26 (June 1967): 161–181.
  30. Paul Ramsey, *Deeds and Rules in Christian Ethics* (New York: Charles Scribner's Sons, 1967), pp. 108–109.
  31. John R. Cavanagh, *"Bene Mori:* The Right of the Patient to Die with Dignity," *Linacre Quarterly* 30 (May 1963): 60–68. This right follows from the traditionally accepted principle that the individual does not have to use extraordinary means to preserve one's life.
  32. Muller, *Studies in Genetics*, p. 590.
  33. Muller, *The Control of Human Heredity and Evolution*, p. 109.
  34. Muller, *The Population Crisis and the Use of World Resources*, p. 332.
  35. H. Richard Niebuhr, *The Kingdom of God in America* (New York: Harper and Row, 1937; Torchbook, 1959), p. 193.
  36. Lederberg, *Bulletin of the Atomic Scientists* 22 (October 1966): 9–10.
  37. E.g., M. Klein, *Man and His Future*, p. 280.
  38. *A.A.S* 45 (1953): 602, 603.
  39. Muller, *The Control of Human Heredity and Evolution*, p. 100.
  40. Muller, *The Population Crisis and the Use of World Resources*, p. 323.
  41. Most of the points briefly mentioned in this third danger have been developed at greater length by Ramsey in various articles and books, although I would again disagree with the eschatology sometimes expressed in these contexts. On consequentialism in general,

see Ramsey, *Deeds and Rules in Christian Ethics,* especially pp. 176–225. For my evaluation of consequentialism see *Themes in Fundamental Moral Theology* (Notre Dame, Ind.: University of Notre Dame Press, 1977), pp. 121–144.

42. *A.A.S.* 45 (1953): 605, 606.

43. William H. van der Marck, O. P., *Toward a Christian Ethic* (Westminster, Md.: Newman Press, 1967), pp. 48–69.

44. Lederberg, *Bulletin of the Atomic Scientists* 22 (October 1966): 10. Ramsey develops the point at great length in his article on cloning.

45. Ramsey, *Genetics and the Future of Man,* pp. 155–157.

PART THREE

Sexual and Medical Ethics in Institutional and Public Policy

6: The Catholic Hospital Code, The Catholic Believer and a Pluralistic Society

Catholic hospitals are often identified as Catholic because they follow the Ethical and Religious Directives for Catholic Health Facilities which were approved by the American bishops in November 1971.[1] In Canada in 1970, the Canadian bishops promulgated a similar set of guidelines, The Medico-Moral Guide.[2]

Today questions are being raised about the hospital code of ethics. Can any changes be made in the code? What about Catholics who might dissent from some of the teachings of the code? What about following the code in a pluralistic setting in which government funds support hospitals and the hospital is expected to serve all people in the area, Catholic as well as non-Catholic? What if following the code would seriously curtail the quality of the medical care given by the Catholic facility or perhaps even force it out of existence?

This chapter will begin by situating the question of the hospital code in the broader context of the health care witness and service of the Catholic Church. Second, the tension of using a moral teaching proposed as a guide for individual conscience as an institutional code will be discussed. Third, the problem arising from a Catholic hospital code in the context of a pluralistic society will be explored and appropriate conclusions drawn.

I. The Hospital Code in the General Context
of Catholic Witness and Service

As a first step it is necessary to understand the question of the hospital code within the broader context of the mission of the Roman Catholic Church and its witness and service to the sick. Care for the sick constitutes a basic Gospel imperative for the individual Christian. The Catholic tradition, for example, sees the care for the sick as one of the corporal works of mercy.

In addition, the Church as a community should give a community witness and service to the care of the sick, but such an apostolate and witness can be accomplished in many different ways. For example, the Church community can organize a group of dedicated Christians in the name of the Church to visit and console the sick. The sacrament of the sick in its own way constitutes an excellent witness to the care and concern for the sick. But there can be many other ways in which such a community or Church apostolate exists. The form of community witness to the care of the sick which is the one we usually think of today involves an institutional witness as such. The health care facility—hospital, clinic or retirement home—as institution is owned and operated by a denomination or church or by a particular group within a church or denomination. Within the past few years there have been discussions about the proper legal incorporation for Catholic or religious institutions, but our concern does not include the legal aspects of incorporation.[3]

Catholic institutional presence in the health care apostolate, especially in the form of Catholic hospitals, has been a very significant and visible aspect of the Roman

Catholic witness and service to the sick. Historically, the Church has been instrumental in setting up and maintaining hospital facilities. Without contradiction, one can state that the Church has been a leader in this field and is generally recognized as such even in the secular world.

However, such institutional witness is not absolutely necessary for the Church to fulfill its community witness and service to the care of the sick. The question of priorities always enters into the determination of what forms of institutional service the Church should provide. There are many criteria which are appropriate in establishing such priorities, but one must always include the real needs of people and the ways in which society is already attempting to meet those needs. In changing historical circumstances, the priorities of institutional Church witness can and even should change. Even today a new form of Church apostolate has emerged in some areas of health care. The Church or a Church organization serves as a catalyst to bring people together and obtain government funding to build and staff nursing homes for senior citizens which are established as private but non-religiously affiliated institutions.

The Church in a process of corporate discernment must constantly strive to ascertain its own priorities in the most fitting form of service in the light of the Gospel and the signs of the times. There can be an ecclesial service, witness and apostolate to the dying without an institutional presence, even though historically the institutional presence has been a very significant part of the Church's witness. One cannot in advance rule out the possibility that the Roman Catholic Church should give up its institutional involvement in hospitals and health facilities for a number of different reasons, including the fact that the Church might not be able to carry out its own ethical commitments in these institutions.

Granted the existence of Catholic hospitals or health care facilities as such, the question naturally arises: What makes such institutions Catholic? Such a question would always be legitimate, but it becomes even more critical in the light of many contemporary events. Religious communities which once staffed Catholic hospitals do not have the number of vocations they had in the past and they may not be able to continue to staff the institutions. Funding today generally comes from public sources. Governmental regulations and planning exert great influences on all hospitals. Many patients and even staff and administrators in Catholic hospitals are not themselves Catholic.

The questioning about the exact identity of a Catholic hospital must also be seen in the light of a broader questioning occurring in the Church today. There have been a number of symposia on the meaning and identity of Catholic colleges and universities.[4] There exists an even more radical questioning about the existence of a specifically Christian ethics and on what precise level of ethical reality there is a specifically Christian ethic.[5]

An attempted solution to the problem of the identity and meaning of a Catholic hospital or health facility lies beyond the scope of this study, but it will be helpful to establish some parameters for this discussion. In the light of the subsequent discussion on the hospital code of ethics, it must be emphasized that the observance of the code alone is not a sufficient source of Catholic identity for the hospitals. Unfortunately, it seems that the Catholic identity of a health care facility was in the past often reduced to the observance of the prescribed Catholic hospital code. Lately, a number of articles have perceptively pointed out the need for something more.[6] Kevin O'Rourke speaks of a threefold aspect to Catholic identity: (1) communicating a message with emphasis on the sacredness of human life, the meaning of suffering and death, and Christ's love for the poor; (2) establishing a community within the hospital; (3) performing service.[7]

In attempting to discern the broader meaning and identity of the Catholic hospital, there are two parameters that must be kept in mind. First, there is a danger of claiming certain things as specific to Catholic identity when they are not. For example, a respect for the human life and concern for the poor are not uniquely Catholic. Elsewhere I have argued that in terms of specific content, conclusions and proximate content dispositions (such as care for the needy, self-sacrificing love), there is no specifically Christian content in ethics. The explicit Christian aspect affects the transcendental aspect of the human act and the areas of motivation and intentionality. This in no way denies that Christian love should become concrete, but non-Christians can arrive at the same conclusions and share the same proximate dispositions, attitudes and values.[8] The second parameter exists in tension with the first. The culture and ethos of any one period are marked also by human limitation, finitude and sinfulness. There is the perennial danger of conforming the Gospel to the contemporary culture. The relationship between Gospel and culture always involves tension. Chapter one pointed out that on the one hand culture may support Gospel values, but on the other hand it might impede the Gospel. Any attempt to describe the meaning of a Catholic institution must be aware of the twofold danger of either claiming too much as specifically Christian or also forgetting that at times the Gospel will be in opposition to the culture.

II. Tensions Arising from Medical-Moral Directives
as Institutional Policy

The first source of tensions to be considered involves the fact that the Ethical and Religious Directives for Catholic Health Facilities apply to institutional policy the moral directives and teaching which the Roman Catholic Church proposes for the conscience of its individual members.[9] Moral directives cannot be transposed from directives for the individual Catholic conscience to institutional policy for a health care facility without some resulting tensions. As directives for the individual Catholic conscience, these norms admit a number of responses which are not now accepted in the area of institutional policy in Catholic health facilities in the United States. All these different responses place heavy emphasis on the person and the subjective aspect of the moral actor, but the existing institutional policy often does not allow such elements to be taken into consideration. The following three aspects will be considered: (1) the concept of invincible ignorance; (2) the possibility of counselling or choosing the lesser of two evils; (3) the right to dissent from authoritative, noninfallible hierarchical teaching.

Invincible Ignorance

Roman Catholic theology has traditionally acknowledged that the human act has a subjective and an objective aspect. The subjective aspect views the human act in its relationship to the person of the subject performing the action, whereas the objective aspect views the act in its relationship to whatever is proposed as the objective moral norm. An act can be objectively wrong, but not subjectively sinful. Legal systems have appropriated the same basic notion by recognizing that wrong actions can be done but subjectively excused because of temporary insanity or some other type of impediment.

The realization of these two aspects of the human act surfaced especially in the historical development of the possibility of invincible ignorance of the natural law. The manuals of moral theology generally acknowledge that there can be invincible ignorance of the more mediate or remote conclusions of the natural law which are deduced from the first principles only through a comparatively long discursive process.[10]

In the context of the debate about probablism St. Alphonsus was attacked for his teaching on the possibility of invincible ignorance of the natural law. Alphonsus's adversaries in this discussion were the Italian Dominican Giovanni Vincenzo Patuzzi, who occasionally used the pen name Adelfo Dositeo, and the anonymous author of *La Regola de'costumi*.[11] Alphonsus maintained that even if one is doubtful about the existence of the natural law obligation, one can still be invincibly ignorant of it. Alphonsus's position rests on two reflex principles. First, doubtful law does not apply because it is not sufficiently promulgated. The second reflex principle maintains that a doubtful law does not oblige. The ultimate metaphysical reasons come from the distinction between the remote law of human acts, which is the divine law, and the dictate of conscience, which is the proximate norm of human actions. By insisting on the proximate norm of human conduct, the essentially voluntary character of the human act, and the intention or the end as the foremost element of the act, St. Alphonsus acknowledges the possibility of an inculpable discrepancy between the remote and proximate norms of human action.[12]

Contemporary Catholic moral theologians have expanded the concept of invincible ignorance. Louis Monden argues that invincible ignorance or error cannot be restricted to a lack of information or a rational grasp of that information but must be expanded to include the whole sphere of psychological incomprehension, unconscious resistance, invincible prejudices, wishful thinking and affective transferences of every kind.[13]

Bernard Häring distinguishes the level of moral theology from the level of pastoral counselling. Häring sees such a distinction in the older approach to invincible ignorance but realizes that invincible ignorance involves more than mere intellectualism. Invincible ignorance refers to the person's inability to realize a moral obligation because of the individual's total experience, the psychological impasses and the whole context of one's life. There exists a law of growth according to which the counsellor might not be able to urge the fullness of the objective norm at the present time but only look for a step forward which the individual can realistically take in the present situation. Häring sees this law of growth in the light of the tension between the demands of objective morality and the subjective possibilities of the person here and now. Häring applies this understanding to a particularly acute case of abortion after rape although he cautions that he would not go so far as to positively advise the person to abort the fetus.[14] Theologians have continued to discuss such an approach and how it either agrees or differs with proposals put forward by some Protestant ethicians in response to the same basic problem.[15] Thus, even in going against an objectively true moral precept, a person might not always be guilty of sin, and in the forum of pastoral counselling such a decision can be accepted in the light of the principle of growth.

In their commentary on the encyclical *Humanae Vitae,*

the Italian bishops in directing their attention to Catholic spouses refer to the law of growth. Christian spouses should not become discouraged. They should remember there are laws of growth in the attainment of virtue, and at times in striving for the ideal one will pass through stages of imperfection.[16] A commentary on the statement of the Italian bishops speaks of a personalistic perception and the pastoral existential aspects of the Christian life which indicate the need to accept a law of growth in these matters.[17]

In dealing with the individual person one can thus distinguish between the level of objective moral norms and the level of pastoral counselling. However, the Ethical and Religious Directives for Catholic Health Facilities do not seem in themselves to make room for such a distinction, which is an accepted part of the Catholic tradition.

Counselling or Choosing the Lesser of Two Evils

Catholic moral theology has debated the question of counselling the lesser of two evils. One opinion claims that such counselling is not permitted. Whoever counsels or persuades to a lesser evil still truly persuades another to do evil, and this is never licit. However, a more common opinion, which was also maintained by St. Alphonsus, permits the counselling of the lesser of two evils when from the circumstances it is obvious that the counsellor is not proposing the lesser evil as something to be done in itself but rather is dissuading the person from doing the greater evil. The object then of the counselling is not the lesser evil to be done but the greater evil to be avoided, even though in the process the lesser evil must be tolerated. In this case it is important to recognize that both evils are acknowledged to be moral evils and the principal actor cannot be dissuaded from doing evil.[18]

What about choosing rather than just counselling the lesser of two evils? Traditional Catholic moral theology, again relying heavily on St. Alphonsus, speaks about the perplexed conscience in which the person believes that sin is involved in the two available alternative actions. One must delay the action and consult with experts to remove the doubt. If the action cannot be put off, then the lesser evil should be chosen. The impression is given that in actuality there is not objective moral evil in both cases, but the individual does not realize this fact. Again, Catholic moral theology upholds the principle that one can never directly do what is morally evil.[19] Such an approach could also be reformulated into a case of expanded invincible ignorance if the person does not existentially appreciate the moral evil involved in the one act.

In this context, the reaction of the French bishops to *Humanae Vitae* poses some interesting questions. According to the statement issued by the French hierarchy, contraception can never be a good, for it is always a disorder. "But persons can be confronted by a true conflict of duty. On this subject we simply recall the constant moral teaching: When one faces a choice of duties, where one cannot avoid an evil whatever be the decision taken, traditional wisdom requires that one seeks before God which is the greater duty. The spouses will decide for themselves after reflecting together with all the care that the grandeur of their conjugal vocation requires."[20]

The exact meaning of the French bishops in my judgment is not clear. They seem to be doing more than merely counselling their people to choose the lesser of two moral evils. Perhaps they are invoking the case of the perplexed conscience, but the traditional interpretation of that maintains that if experts declare that both actions are intrinsically wrong (to use the terminology of the manuals), then the individual may not do what is intrinsically wrong. Perhaps they are in some way expanding the traditional concept of the perplexed conscience. Perhaps they are merely applying here an expanded concept of invincible ignorance which subjectively excuses the action of the person. Perhaps they are invoking a newer moral principle that contraception in this case is only a physical or premoral evil which can be justified for a proportionate reason.

Is there any way of coping on an institutional level with the problems arising from the fact that on a pastoral level the law of growth or the counselling or choosing of the lesser of two evils might mean that an individual Catholic could, without subjective guilt, do an action which is proscribed by the moral code? One possible way of trying to solve this difficulty can be found in the preamble which the Canadian bishops affixed to their moral guide: "The guidelines present a concise statement of these exigencies in the field of hospital work. They should be read and understood not as commands imposed from without but as demands of the inner dynamism of human and Christian life. And precisely because they are that, their application for a particular situation will usually entail a great deal of prudence and wisdom. There, then, personal conscience will find its field of competence. The guidelines should serve to enlighten this judgment of conscience. They cannot replace it."

One could interpret this paragraph as acknowledging the two types of problems discussed above and recognizing that in practice, at least in some cases, the personal conscience might without guilt come to decisions in which the externally imposed objective norm is not fulfilled. Such an understanding of the hospital code of ethics would allow for approaches on a pastoral level which have been traditionally acknowledged as possible for the individual but which have not been allowed in Catholic health facilities following the letter of the Ethical Directives as proposed by the American bishops. There would be problems in implementing such approaches, but recognition in theory of such pastoral approaches should serve as the framework for trying to work out practical norms for the implementation.

Legitimate Dissent

In the context of the reaction to the encyclical *Humanae Vitae,* many Roman Catholics became aware for the first time that there existed in the Roman Catholic Church the possibility of dissent from authoritative or authentic, noninfallible hierarchical teaching on moral questions. This is the type of teaching generally found in the guidelines or codes proposed for Catholic health facilities. Even some national bishops' conferences acknowledged that after study and reflection a Catholic could dissent from the encyclical's teaching on contraception.[21]

In speaking about those who cannot accept the encyclical's teaching on some points, the Canadian bishops pointed out: "Since they are not denying any point of divine or Catholic faith nor rejecting the teaching authority of the Church, these Catholics should not be considered or consider themselves shut off from the body of the faithful. But they should remember that their good faith will be dependent upon a sincere self-examination to determine the true motives and grounds for such suspension of assent and on continued effort to understand and deepen their knowledge of the teaching of the Church."[22] Note that the Canadian bishops themselves do not dissent from the encyclical teaching, but they acknowledge the explicit right of Catholics to dissent.

The debate about dissent in the Roman Catholic Church from specific teachings of the authentic or authoritative, noninfallible hierarchical magisterium continues. The ultimate theological reasons for such dissent can be reduced to two: (1) from the epistemological perspective, on such specific issues one cannot obtain the type of certitude that excludes the possibility of error; (2) from the ecclesiogical perspective, the whole teaching and learning function of the Roman Catholic Church cannot be totally identified with the hierarchical teaching office of the Church. In my judgment, dissent is now and will be a more frequent occurrence in the Church, but not all agree.[23] At least in theory one has to maintain within the Roman Catholic Church the possibility of dissent from such authentic or authoritative, noninfallible Church teaching.

At the present time in the United States the most significant issue in the area of medical morality and the hospital code involves direct sterilization. Directives 18 and 20 of the Ethical and Religious Directives for Catholic Health Facilities spell out the prohibition of direct sterilization which has been presented by the authoritative hierarchical teaching: "Sterilization, whether permanent or temporary, for man or for woman, may not be used as a means of contraception." This same prohibition is found in the Medico-Moral Guide proposed in 1970 by the Canadian bishops.[24]

The Directives, passed by the American bishops in November 1971, contain a charge to the Committee on Health Affairs of the United States Catholic Conference, using the widest consultation possible, to review suggestions from the field and to discuss periodically the need for an updated revision of the Directives. A committee was set up for this purpose. The topic of sterilization was discussed, but there were great divisions within the committee on this issue including the theologians who were members of the committee. The matter was brought to the attention of the Administrative Board of the National Conference of Catholic Bishops. A special review committee studied the issue, and it was decided in 1973 to send the issue to Rome for guidance. Both written and oral presentations were made to Rome early in 1974. On April 14, 1975, Archbishop Joseph Bernardin, President of the National Conference of Catholic Bishops, sent a letter to all bishops informing them that the question of sterilization had been examined at length including consultation with the Holy See. He writes: ". . . to give assurance that the 1971 Guidelines stand as written and that direct sterilization is not to be considered as justified by the common good, the principle of totality, the existence of contrary opinion, or any other argument. This means that Catholic hospitals, as a matter of institutional policy, may not authorize sterilization procedures for reasons other than those contained in the guidelines. If questions of material cooperation arise, the traditional norms of moral theology are to be applied."

On December 4, 1975, Bishop James S. Rausch, then general secretary of the National Conference of Catholic Bishops, sent to all American bishops a response from the Doctrinal Congregation dated March 13, 1975. This document was obviously the basis of Archbishop Bernardin's earlier letter. The document of the Doctrinal Congregation recognizes the dissent against this teaching from many theologians but "denies that doctrinal significance can be attributed to the fact as such so as to constitute a 'theological source' which the faithful might invoke and thereby abandon the authentic magisterium, and follow the opinions of private theologians which dissent from it."[25]

There exists a significant dissent from this teaching proscribing direct sterilization, even though some do not acknowledge their position as a form of dissent. Many Roman Catholic theologians have publicly justified the right to dissent from such teaching condemning direct sterilization.[26] The dissent also exists in practice. The *Policy Manual* of St. Joseph's Hospital, London, Ontario, acknowledges "in certain cases where the total medical health of a woman may be gravely jeopardized by a future pregnancy, a tubal ligation may be considered objectively a moral act different from a tubal ligation done where there are no grave medical complications."[27] The policy for Catholic hospitals in Manitoba, Canada, also permits sterilization for serious medical reasons.[28] In many hospitals in the province of Ontario, Canada, sterilizations are performed.[29] In the United States there has also been much discussion on the issue of sterilization. A number of Catholic hospitals have been permitting sterilization under conditions often based on those used at St. Joseph's Hospital in London, Ontario. Some hospitals have solved the problem by leaving the decision to a committee without any developed criteria proposed for the guidance of the committee.[30]

In my judgment sterilization involves basically the same moral issues as contraception. Whoever dissents from the teaching on contraception logically must also dissent from the prohibition of direct sterilization. The only difference is that sterilization tends to be permanent, and there should be a more permanent or serious reason to justify it. Consequently, sterilization if permitted cannot be restricted just to medical reasons, but any truly human reason which is of proportionate serious-ness suffices—sociological, psychological, economic or other.

The recent letter of Archbishop Bernardin and the document from the Doctrinal Congregation do not take away the legitimacy of dissent for a Roman Catholic. One must be open to the teaching of these documents, but the documents themselves claim only to be repeat-ing the traditional teaching as already enunciated. If, after prayerful and thoughtful consideration, one has already dissented from such teaching, such dissent can continue to be a legitimate option for the loyal Roman Catholic.[31]

It is now necessary to address a question which heretofore has not received enough attention—the limits of dissent. The Commission of the Catholic Theological Society of America, of which I was a member, acknowledged the right to dissent and talked about its applications in the areas covered by the hospi-tal code. However, the Commission did not delve deeply into the very significant question of the limits of dissent with regard to the hospital code.[32] It is this important question which now needs to be addressed.

In the realm of practical reality the question is often phrased: If it is legitimate for a Roman Catholic to dis-sent on contraception and sterilization, is it also legiti-mate to dissent on abortion and euthanasia? Already there are some Roman Catholic theologians who are questioning the traditional teaching and dissenting from it in the areas both of abortion and euthanasia.[33] At the present time the sterilization issue seems to be the one which is receiving all the attention, but is this merely the foot in the door? Once the sterilization issue is solved and direct sterilization is permitted in Catholic hospitals, then will abortion and euthanasia follow?

The reasons briefly mentioned justifying the possibility of dissent from authoritative, authentic, noninfallible Church teaching are also present with regard to the possibility of dissent on abortion and on euthanasia. Legitimate dissent in these areas remains a possibility because of the complexity and specificity of the material with which we are dealing and the fact that one cannot obtain the degree of certitude that excludes the possibility of error. One can, and in my judgment must, apply to those denying the hierarchical teaching on abortion and euthanasia what the Canadian bishops said about those dissenting from *Humanae Vitae:* "Since they are not denying any point of divine and Catholic faith nor rejecting the teaching authority of the Church, these Catholics should not be considered, or consider themselves, shut off from the body of the faithful." For this reason I have urged that ultimate Roman Catholic identity cannot be sought in terms of absolute acceptance of specific moral teachings, including the teaching on abortion and euthanasia.

Although dissent from specific moral teachings always remains a possibility for the individual Roman Catholic, this does not mean that such dissent is always justified and right. There must be reasons to justify the dissent, but this does not limit dissent only to theologians. Theology by definition operates on the level of the systematic, the thematic and the reflexive, but every Christian can and must arrive at ethical judgments. The ordinary Christian makes decisions in a nonthematic, nonreflexive and nonsystematic way, but these are not pejorative terms. One does not have to be a theologian in order to be able to dissent from hierarchical teaching, but prudence calls for one to seek out how theologians and other people in the Church have approached the particular point in question.

However, if one emphasizes only the possibility of dissent on specific moral questions, then it becomes impossible for the Church or its teaching to take on any incarnational existence in a given historical time and place. The historical Roman Catholic community cannot be restricted merely to the realm of infallible or of *de fide* statements. If this were true, it would overly restrict the existence of the Church as a community which should have an incarnational existence in time and place. Catholic identity would be reduced to a small, ahistorical core in much the same way as liberal theology reduced the core or essence of Christianity. The dilemma involves the classical case of the rights of the individual and the legitimate needs of the community. There must be a way in which both aspects are given their due.

In the historical reality of human and Christian existence, Roman Catholic moral teaching and identity can be gauged by the reaction of the whole Church in its teaching and in its learning as well as in its living. Not only the teaching of the hierarchical magisterium but also the praxis of the community and the teaching of theologians must be considered. It is always difficult to assess adequately the praxis of the whole Church, but the difficulty does not eliminate the importance and significance of the norm. The historical self-identification and praxis of the Church in any given moment never furnish an absolute criterion of truth; but, nonetheless, it is the only acceptable norm of the identity of the historical community as such. A conflict between the conscientious belief of the individual Catholic and the praxis of the historical Church community remains possible, and such a conflict merely mirrors the tension which will always exist within the Church community between the community itself and the individual.

Praxis itself has changed on some matters and might change in the future. Thirty years ago one could not appeal to any practice against the teaching of the Roman Catholic Church on sterilization, but today in my judgment one can. The method of determining the praxis of the Church at any one given time cannot be reduced just to a majority vote. One is here trying to discern the work of the Spirit in and through the praxis of the Church. In this context one must pay significant attention to all the aspects of the Church. Where there begins to be a change in the praxis of the Church on a particular teaching, the tension and conflict will become more acute.

At the present time I do not think that the praxis of the Church on most aspects of the questions of abortion and euthanasia differs from the teaching of the hierarchical magisterium. (I say "most aspects" because it seems that at the present time the older application of the theory of double effect to conflict situations involving abortion is not accepted in the praxis of the Church, as illustrated in the Church's forbidding abortion of the fetus to save the life of the mother.) Personally I have proposed positions which dissent to some extent from the teaching of the hierarchical magisterium on abortion and euthanasia. Other Roman Catholic theologians have proposed opinions which dissent even more from that teaching, but at the present time the praxis of the Roman Catholic Church does not seem to have moved away from the accepted teachings. The process of discerning the praxis of the total Church will always be difficult, but in this way one tries to balance the rights of the individual member of the Church and the life of the community incarnated in the historical times and culture of a given period. Thus one could conclude that the institutional policy of Catholic hospitals today should allow sterilizations, but that does not entail the general acceptance of abortion or euthanasia.

III. Tensions Arising from the Pluralistic Context

A second source of tension involves the pluralistic society in which Catholic institutions exist. Many Catholic hospitals serve non-Catholic patients as well as Catholic patients. Catholic hospitals like other private hospitals often receive various forms of government funding. How is the Catholic health facility with its institutional code of ethics to relate to these other persons who do not subscribe to such an ethical code?

There are a number of pressing practical dilemmas which illustrate the types of problems that can and have arisen. At the present time in the United States the most pressing problems are associated with sterilization (tubal ligation) and affect both large hospitals in metropolitan areas and hospitals in smaller communities. In large Catholic hospitals in metropolitan areas physicians with privileges at the Catholic hospital often have privileges at other hospitals where they will do tubal ligations. Multiple staff appointments erode the obstetricians' loyalty to the Catholic hospital. Time pressures, exacerbated by transportation problems, may force doctors to concentrate most of their practice in institutions which allow the performance of all accepted operations and procedures including tubal ligations. The loss of good ob/gyn staff will also have repercussions on the quality of medical care offered at the Catholic hospital. Expertise will be lacking for other specialties. No one service—medicine, surgery, pediatrics, ob/gyn—exists in a vacuum. If the hospital is a teaching hospital with medical and nursing education units, its very existence could be threatened.

Problems also exist on the level of smaller communities. Regional health planning units are now organizing health care in particular areas. Often the Catholic hospital might be the designated place for ob/gyn, but the refusal to do tubal ligations often prevents a Catholic institution from having such a unit for the total area. If Catholic institutions are unable to allow such operations, they will lose their ob/gyn units and perhaps put their total existence in jeopardy.

Another illustration involves the situation where the Catholic hospital is the only hospital in the area. What then about the rights of non-Catholics in that particular area? Is it just and fair that they cannot have the medical operations which good medical practice calls for, at least in the eyes of the individuals and their physicians? Legal cases have been brought against Catholic hospitals for refusing to do abortions and sterilizations, but final decisions have ruled in favor of the hospitals.[34]

Two important generic considerations shed light on possible solutions to these cases: the question of cooperation and the question of pluralism in our society.

Cooperation

The older approach understood cooperation in terms of cooperating with an act which is wrong. On the basis of a more personalistic understanding and in the light of the newer approach to the question of conscience and religious liberty, I have proposed a different theory of cooperation. One does not cooperate with an act which is wrong but rather with a person who is usually convinced that the action is good.[35]

In the question of religious liberty, contemporary Catholic teaching expressed in the Second Vatican Council recognizes that individuals should be free to act in accord with the dictates of their conscience in religious matters—that is, they should be free from external coercion which prevents them from acting in the way they want or forces them to act in a way contrary to their conscientious conviction. The approach to religious liberty within Roman Catholicism was changed precisely because it was recognized that in this case one is not cooperating with an act which is intrinsically wrong, but rather with a person who has in religious matters the civil and juridical right to act in accord with one's own conscience in these matters.

Even in the matter of religious liberty (which as a civil and moral right is not exactly the same as the moral right of a person to act in accord with a sincere conscience), there are certain limits placed on that liberty. In the juridical order the state can intervene and restrict the exercise of religious liberty on the basis of the criterion of public order, which embraces an order of peace, of justice and of morality (Declaration on Religious Freedom, par. n. 7). Our life with others in a pluralistic society should follow the same basic approach. Often in our society we must cooperate in some way with others with whom we are in disagreement. Limits to our cooperation should be based on the same criterion of the public order with its threefold aspect of an order of peace, of justice and of basic morality necessary for living in society. We thus respect the rights of others in our society to perform certain actions, but one can refuse to cooperate if the action in the judgment of personal conscience interferes with the public order, especially the rights of others.

Within the parameters of this approach a proportionate reason is necessary to justify the cooperation, but often I would judge that the rights of the other person could constitute such a reason, although some might demand a stronger reason to justify the person who cooperates in an act thought to be morally wrong but not harmful to the public order. Such an approach to cooperation tries to respect all the many values present in the situation—the conscience and rights of the principal actor, the conscience and rights of the cooperator and the effect of the act on others and on society.

What about the cooperation of a Catholic hospital in operations and procedures which are opposed to Catholic teaching? In a true sense the hospital as a moral or legal person does not perform operations, but allows them to be done. It would seem that even weaker reasons are required to justify cooperation in this case, but the meaning of cooperation by a legal or moral person needs greater study. Applying the principles of cooperation outlined above, the Catholic hospital is justified in permitting sterilization and other procedures which do not harm the public order when there are sufficient reasons such as a serious violation of the rights of others. However, the Catholic hospital ordinarily could refuse to perform abortions or other procedures which are judged to take human life, thereby going against the rights of others and public order.

Pluralistic Society

A second consideration involves the functioning of pluralism in society. If possible, society should foster and encourage the right of peoples or groups to act according to their conscientious convictions. In practice such a principle means that individuals or groups should not be forced to cooperate (as distinguished from voluntary cooperation considered above) in actions which they deem to be wrong. However, this principle of encouraging groups to act in accord with their own conscientious convictions obviously exists alongside other values. Conflicts will arise when the rights of some groups and individuals to act in accord with the dictates of their consciences collide with the rights of other people to act in accord with their consciences.

In many cases, especially in large urban areas, society can foster this pluralism without curtailing the rights of others. Catholic hospitals coexist together with non-Catholic hospitals. Catholic hospitals can adhere to their institutional ethical code without harming the rights of others who have easy access to other health facilities. Conflicts can become more acute in situations involving the consolidation and coordination of health care facilities, which is taking place not only in small areas but even in urban areas. Acute problems also exist where the Catholic health facility is the only one serving a particular area.

As already mentioned in the consideration of cooperation, it seems that Catholic hospitals can and should, where necessary, cooperate in operations such as sterilization and other operations in which there is no harm being done to other innocent persons. Within civil society, everything possible should be done to support the conscientious decisions of individuals not to participate in what they believe to be the taking of human life. The primary purpose of human society is to protect and enhance human life, which is a most fundamental value in society. If at all possible, individuals and groups within society should not be forced to engage in, or cooperate with, what they believe to be the morally wrong taking of life. This fundamental line of reason also argues for the need for selective conscientious objection to military service. For example, the bishops of the United States have issued a statement urging such selective conscientious objection precisely because of the fact that unjust war involves the wrong taking of life.[36] Whenever one believes that human life is wrongly being taken, the state should go as far as possible to see that such a conscience is protected. It could be that at times it will be impossible to do this, but cooperation in such matters should be required only as a last resort.

Conclusion

This study has touched on the meaning of the Catholic identity of health care facilities and examined the problems connected with the institutional Catholic medico-moral code resulting from two different sources. Often the problems will overlap so that one could justify direct sterilization in Catholic hospitals either on the basis of dissent or counselling the lesser of two evils or on the basis of cooperation. To avoid the problem resulting from the fact that norms for the individual conscience are now posed as institutional policy, it should be recognized in the hospital code that these norms are to be applied and interpreted in the light of accepted pastoral practices and interpretations. To solve the problems resulting from the pluralistic nature of the contemporary situation, the principle of cooperation should be applied as explained above. In all these matters there will still be tensions, but the application and interpretation of the suggested approaches should be worked out on the local level in the light of the existing circumstances.

NOTES

1. These directives may be obtained from the Department of Health Affairs, United States Catholic Conference, 1312 Massachusetts Avenue, N.W., Washington, D.C. 20005. They may also be found in John F. Dedek, *Contemporary Medical Ethics* (New York: Sheed and Ward, 1975), pp. 206–214.

2. This guide may be obtained from the Catholic Hospital Association of Canada, 312 Daly Avenue, Ottawa, Canada. Also found in Dedek, pp. 201–205.

3. E.g., John Joseph McGrath, *Catholic Institutions in the United States: Canonical and Civil Law Status* (Washington, D.C.: Catholic University of America Press, 1968); Adam J. Maida, *Ownership, Control and Sponsorship of Catholic Institutions* (Harrisburg, Pa.: Pennsylvania Catholic Conference, 1975). Eugene J. Schulte, et al., "Strategies for Preserving Individual and Corporate Rights," *Hospital Progress* 55 (February 1974): 52–68.

4. *The Catholic University: A Modern Appraisal,* ed. Neil J. McCluskey (Notre Dame, Ind.: University of Notre Dame Press, 1970); Frederick J. Crosson, "How is a College Catholic in Practice?" *Delta Epsilon Sigma Bulletin* 20, no. 2 (May 1975): 54–59; James F. Hitchcock, "How is a College or University Catholic in Practice?" *Delta Epsilon Sigma Bulletin* 20, no. 2 (May 1975): 40–53.

5. For an opinion denying the existence of a specifically distinctive content in Christian ethics, see Josef Fuchs, *Human Values and Christian Morality* (Dublin: Gill and Macmillan, 1970), especially pp. 112–147; Fuchs, "Gibt es eine spezifisch christliche Moral?" *Stimmen der Zeit* 95 (1970): 526–550; Fuch, "Esiste una morale non-cristiana?" *Rassegna di teologia* 14 (1973): 361–373. For a different approach, see James M. Gustafson, *Can Ethics Be Christian?* (Chicago: University of Chicago Press, 1975).

6. E.g., "A Symposium: The Future Model of the Catholic Hospital," *Hospital Progress* 55 (October 1974): 41–60.

7. Kevin D. O'Rourke, "Is Your Health Facility Catholic?" *Hospital Progress* 55 (April 1974): 40–44.

8. "Is There a Catholic and/or Christian Ethic?" *Proceedings of the Catholic Theological Society of America* 29 (1974): 125–154. Note the responses by James M. Gustafson and Richard A. McCormick.

9. The questions treated here and in the following section have been raised by others. See Warren T. Reich, "Policy vs. Ethics," *Linacre Quarterly* 39 (1972): 21–29; also, "The Report of the Commission on Ethical and Religious Directives for Catholic Hospitals Commissioned by the Board of Directors of the Catholic Theological Society of America," *Proceedings of the Catholic Theological Society of America* 27 (1972): 242–269. For a negative critique of the above report, see Donald J. Keefe, "A Review and Critique of the CTSA Report," *Hospital Progress* 54 (February 1973): 57–69. In the remainder of this article I will develop in greater detail some ideas proposed and discussed in these earlier writings.

10. Stanley Bertke, *The Possibility of Invincible Ignorance of the Natural Law* (Washington, D.C.: Catholic University of America Press, 1941).

11. Adelfo Dositeo [Giovanni Vincenzo Patuzzi], *La Causa del probabilismo richiamata all'esame da Monsignor D. Alfonso de Liguori e convinta novellamente di falsitá* (Ferrara: Remondini, 1764), Chap. V, p. 60; Chap. X, p. 142; Adelfo Dositeo, *Osservazioni teologiche sopra l'Apologia dell' Illustriss. e Reverendiss. Monsig. D. Alfonso de Liguori contro il libro intitolato La Causa del probabilismo ec.* (Ferrara: Remondini, 1765), Chap. VII, pp. 115–117.

12. Alfonso de'Liguori, *Apologia in cui si difende la Dissertazione del medesimo prima data in luce circa l'uso moderato dell'opinione probabile dalle opposizioni fattegli da un molto Rev. P. Lettore che si nomina Adelfo Dositeo* (Venice: Remondini, 1764); Alfonso de'Liguori, *Dell'uso moderato dell'opinione probabile* (Naples: Giuseppe di Domenico, 1765).

13. Louis Monden, *Sin, Liberty and Law* (New York: Sheed and Ward, 1965), p. 138.

14. Bernard Häring, "A Theological Evaluation," in *The Morality of Abortion: Legal and Historical Perspectives,* ed. John T. Noonan, Jr. (Cambridge: Harvard University Press, 1970), pp. 139–142. Also see Häring, *Medical Ethics* (Notre Dame, Ind.: Fides Publishers, 1973), pp. 112–115.

15. Häring was originally responding to the solution proposed by James M. Gustafson, "A Protestant Ethical Approach," in Noonan, pp. 101–122. For further discussions about abortion in this case, see Stanley Hauerwas, *Vision and Virtue: Essays in Christian Ethical Reflection* (Notre Dame, Ind.: Fides Publishers, 1974), pp. 158–164; Richard A. McCormick, "Notes on Moral Theology," *Theological Studies* 35 (1974): 339–342.

16. "Il communicato della Conferenza Episcopale Italiana," in *Presenza pastorale* 39 (January-February 1969): 49. An English trans-

lation can be found in William A. Shannon, *The Lively Debate: Response to Humanae Vitae* (New York: Sheed and Ward, 1970), p. 124.

17. Ambrogio Valsecchi, "Commento," *Presenze pastorale* 39 (January-February 1969): 51–52.

18. I. Aertnys, C. Damen, *Theologia Moralis*, 17th ed., ed. J. Visser (Rome: Marietti, 1956), I, no. 379, p. 366.

19. H. Noldin, A. Schmitt, *Summa Theologiae Moralis: De Principiis*, 33d ed., ed. G Heinzel (Oeniponte: Rauch, 1960), I, no. 214, p. 203; Aertnys-Damen, no. 70, p. 81.

20. National Catholic News Service (Foreign), November 9, 1968. "Note pastorale de l'episcopat français sur 'Humanae Vitae,'" *Documentation Catholique* 65 (1968): 2060.

21. Shannon (pp. 145, 146) puts the statements of the following episcopal conferences under this category—Austrian, Belgian, Canadian, Dutch, French, Scandanavian.

22. National Catholic News Service (Foreign), September 30, 1968.

23. Thomas Dubay, "The State of Moral Theology: A Critical Appraisal," *Theological Studies* 35 (1974): 482–506. For my response to Dubay, see "Pluralism in Catholic Moral Theology," *Chicago Studies* 14 (1975): 310–334.

24. Article 18 of the Canadian Guide condemns sterilization as a means of birth control. Article 19 condemns artificial contraception employing a citation from *Humanae Vitae;* but an N. B. is added in italics: "Reference should be made to the Canadian bishops' documents on the pastoral application of this general direction." Logically, the statement of the Canadian bishops in which they acknowledge the rightful possibility of dissent from *Humanae Vitae* should also apply to direct sterilization which is condemned when "used as a means of birth control."

25. The document issued on March 13 and signed by Cardinal Seper, the Prefect of the Doctrinal Congregation, and Archbishop Hamer, its Secretary, is entitled: "Documentum circa Sterilizationem in Nosocomiis Catholicis: Responsa ad Quaesita Conferentiae Episcopalis Americae Septentrionalis" (prot. 2027/69).

26. Quentin de la Bedoyere, "Sterilization and Human Reason," *New Blackfriars* 48 (1966/67): 153–156; Franz Böckle, "Ethische Aspekte der freiwilligen operativen Sterilisation," *Stimmen der Zeit* 192 (1974): 755–760; Charles E. Curran, "Sterilization: Roman Catholic Theory and Practice," *Linacre Quarterly* 40 (1973): 97–108; Dedek, pp. 72–76; Häring, *Medical Ethics*, pp. 90–91; Richard A. McCormick, "Medico-Moral Questions: Vasectomy and Sterilization," *Linacre Quarterly* 38 (1971): 7–10; Thomas A. Wassmer, *Christian Ethics for Today* (Milwaukee: Bruce Publishing Co., 1969), pp. 174–192. For an opinion denying the right to dissent on sterilization, see

Thomas A. O'Donnell, "Hospital Directives: A Crisis in Faith," *Linacre Quarterly* 39 (1972): 143. For a random sampling of Catholic medical opinion opposed to sterilization, see Eugene F. Diamond, "Clinical Medico-Moral Issues Regarding Sterilization," *Linacre Quarterly* 42 (1975): 6–13. For a complete bibliography, see the 1974 edition of the *Policy Manual* mentioned in the following note.

27. *Policy Manual for Committee to Advise on Requests for Obstetrical/ Gynaecological Sterilization Procedures* (London, Ontario, Canada: St. Joseph's Hospital, 1973), p. 11.

28. *Medico-Moral Policy: Province of Manitoba* (Catholic Hospital Conference of Manitoba, 1970), art. 18.

29. Gladys Shirley Young, "Family Life Services in Catholic Hospitals in Ontario," (M.A. thesis, School of Hygiene at the University of Toronto, 1975).

30. Anthony R. Kosnik, "The Present Status of the Ethical and Religious Directives for Catholic Health Facilities," *Linacre Quarterly* 40 (1973): 84–90.

31. I would strongly dissent from the document of the Doctrinal Congregation if the excerpt cited in the text precludes the legitimacy of dissent in theory and in practice from the condemnation of direct sterilization. All Catholics must admit in theory the possibility of dissent. Perhaps the Congregation is merely saying that in its prudential judgment the reasons for dissent do not exist in this case. Perhaps it would allow for the possibility of dissent but not in such a way that theological dissent becomes a "theological source" which the faithful might invoke against the authentic magisterium.

32. *Report of the Commission*, nn. 44, 59–64.

33. For diverse positions on abortion within Roman Catholicism, see *Theological Studies* 31 (March 1970): 1–176; *Abtreibung—Pro und Contra*, ed. J. Gründel (Wurzburg: Echter, 1971); *Avortement et respect de la vie humaine*, Colloque du Centre Catholique des Médecins Français (Paris: Éditions du Seuil, 1972); L. Babbini et al., *Aborto: questione aperta* (Turin: Gribaldi, 1973). On euthanasia, see Daniel C. Maguire, *Death by Choice* (Garden City, N.Y.: Doubleday, 1974).

34. Eugene J. Schulte, "Challenges to Individual and Corporate Rights," *Hospital Progress* 55 (February 1974): 52–56; Schulte, "Review of Legal Challenges to Catholic Hospitals," *Hospital Progress* 56 (April 1975): 10, 11.

35. Charles E. Curran, "Cooperation: Toward a Revision of the Concept and its Application," *Linacre Quarterly* 41 (1974): 152–167.

36. United States Catholic Conference, "Declaration on Conscientious Objection and Selective Conscientious Objection," October 21, 1971.

7: Population Control: Methods and Morality

Population control and family planning are related, but at the same time quite distinct. Family planning involves the decisions and activities of husbands and wives to plan the size of their families in the light of their responsibilities, obligations, needs and desires. Reasons for family planning, such as those proposed by Pope Pius XII in 1951—medical, eugenic, economic and social indications—are much broader and more inclusive than factors affecting population. Even if there were no need for population control, there would still be need for family planning. Population control is implemented by family planning and many other means, and it involves various organizations and the state itself in planning the optimum population for a given area or even for the earth as a whole.[1]

Population control presupposes there is a population problem and that some control is necessary. As will be mentioned later, the population crisis is more complex than often implied and might more accurately be described as population crises. In addition there are divergent opinions about the gravity of the population problem at the present time, but in my judgment one must admit a problem exists to some extent now, is more acute in developing countries and will become much more serious because in the finite human world in which we live the population cannot continue to increase every year. According to the World Population Plan of Action adopted by the World Population Congress meeting in Bucharest in August 1974 under the auspices of the United Nations, if the world population growth continues at the rate of 2 percent, which has been occurring since 1950, there will be a doubling of the world population every thirty-five years.[2] Despite disagreement about the intensity of the problem, there is need now for some control of population. This raises the questions about the morality of the methods of population control which in some way involve the rights of individuals, families and nations in the light of broader societal and even global needs. From a theological-ethical perspective, there are four preliminary considerations that will influence the approach taken to population control.

Preliminary Theological-Ethical Considerations

1. Harmony or Chaos

Does one generally see in the world the possibility of harmony and order among all the component aspects of human existence, or is one more inclined to see these different aspects as competing forces which very often threaten chaos and disorder? An emphasis on harmony and order has generally characterized much of Roman Catholic moral theology. A most fundamental question in Christian ethics concerns the proper relationship involving love of God, love of neighbor and love of self. The Roman Catholic tradition has tried to harmonize all three of these kinds of love and does not see any opposi-

tion among them if they are properly understood.
Other traditions in Christian ethics have downplayed
the love of self and see self-love as opposed to love for
the neighbor, especially the neighbor in need. Some
would even accuse the Roman Catholic approach as
exemplified in Thomas Aquinas of a eudaemonistic
ethic which in the last analysis is seeking the ultimate
happiness and fulfillment of the individual person.[3]

Pope John XXIII in the second sentence of his encyclical *Pacem in Terris* testifies to the emphasis within the
Roman Catholic tradition on order and harmony in the
world: "The progress of learning and the inventions of
technology clearly show that, both in living things and in
the forces of nature, an astonishing order reigns, and
they also bear witness to the greatness of man who can
understand that order and create suitable instruments
to harness those forces of nature and use them to his
benefit."[4] Such an approach recognizes two different
aspects to this harmony—a basic order in nature itself
but also the rational control of human beings over nature. It would constitute a perversion of this understanding to claim that human beings should never interfere and that a laissez-faire approach will be sufficient.
Nevertheless, this Roman Catholic approach acknowledges a basic order in nature and assumes that the controlling power of human reason can assure that harmony results.

My own approach modifies and qualifies such an
understanding of the order and harmony existing
among the various aspects of human existence. From a
theological perspective, a greater appreciation of sin
and the recognition that the fullness of the eschaton is
not yet here call for the existence of stronger opposed
forces bringing about a greater tension in the world.
From a philosophical perspective, a more historical and

process understanding will also introduce more movement and change, thereby not accepting as much order and harmony as in an older, more static approach. From the perspective of human experience, the tragedy of war, the inequities existing in our world, the divisions existing within many nations, the recognition that many people have died because of famine, the pollution of the environment and many other problems all indicate there are more tensions and possible sources of discord in our world than the first approach is willing to acknowledge.

A third approach sees nature and the world primarily in terms of antagonisms and oppositions so that individuals are opposed to one another, individuals and society are in basic opposition and the forces at work in all of nature are often antithetical and disharmonious. These three different world-views affect not only the general understanding of our world, but also the approach to the question of population control. The third approach more easily despairs of finding any harmonious solution. The competing forces involved in the question of population control are so antagonistic that very radical solutions are necessary.

It is significant that the Roman Catholic hierarchical magisterium has at times been very reluctant to admit the existence of a population problem.[5] Since the encyclical *Populorum Progressio* of Pope Paul VI in 1967, there have been indications that the hierarchical magisterium is willing to recognize to some degree a population problem;[6] but in his address to the World Food Congress on November 19, 1974, Pope Paul did not even acknowledge that there is a problem calling for population control.[7] There is no doubt that a strong factor behind the unwillingness of the Catholic hierarchical magisterium to admit the problem or the gravity of the problem of population stems from its condemnation of artificial contraception. In theory one can separate the two issues (rhythm can be used to secure a lower birth rate), but in practice it is generally recognized that any effective population control on a worldwide basis in our contemporary society must include the use of artificial contraception. However, the refusal of the hierarchical magisterium of the Roman Catholic Church to admit a population problem or the intensity of the problem is consistent with the world-view which stresses the astonishing order and harmony that exist in the world.

My own position is more disposed to accept the existence of a problem such as population but it does not readily endorse drastic and radical solutions. There exists a possibility of harmonizing the different values and forces at work without having to sacrifice totally some of these values or some of the persons involved. Practical solutions will always call for some sacrifice but radical solutions should not be that necessary. With education, motivation, some important structural changes and the ready availability of contraception, human beings will begin to respond to cut down on the number of their offspring.

2. *The Understanding of the State*

In one Christian perspective the state owes its existence primarily to human sinfulness. Sinful human beings will tend to destroy and devour one another unless they are prevented from doing so by a superior force. The state is an order of preservation by which God in accord with the Noachic covenant prevents chaos and preserves some order in this sinful world. The state is understood primarily in terms of coercive power, and the individual's freedom is generally viewed in opposition to the state and to the powers of the state.[8]

Traditional Roman Catholic theology sees the state as a natural society. Human beings are by nature not only social but also political; that is, they are called by nature to join in a political society to work for the common good which ultimately redounds to the good of the individual. Individuals by themselves are not able to achieve some things which are necessary for their good, but by banding together in political society they are able to accomplish these things. A harmony exists between the individual good and the common good. Coercive power is not the primary characteristic of the state because the state has the function of directing and guiding individuals to the common good which ultimately serves for their own good. The state is not viewed as antithetical to the true freedom of the individual.[9]

In practice, there is no doubt that until this present century Roman Catholic theology and philosophy of the state did not give enough importance to the freedom of the individual. With a strong confidence in the ability of the state to discern objective truth and justice, such an approach saw little or no infringement on the freedom of the individual. The freedom of the individual calls for the person to correspond to objective truth and justice.[10] Witness the teaching on religious freedom in the Roman Catholic tradition and the opposition to freedom in general in newer forms of government in the nineteenth century.[11] There is no doubt that the older Roman Catholic approach in the name of objective truth and justice did not give enough importance to the reality of human freedom.

In the light of totalitarian dictatorships in the twentieth century Roman Catholic social ethics has come to give more importance to human freedom and to the human subject.[12] I agree with this approach and with the fact that one cannot so readily insist on objective truth and our ability to know it. In addition, one must also recognize here the effects of the presence of sin because of which the individual will not always be willing to work for the common good and because of which the various powers existing within society might be abused by those who hold them. Such a view of the state recognizes at times the need for coercion and the proper place of coercion in the life of civil society. Free human beings by all means possible should be educated and motivated to work for the common good and the good of society which ultimately redounds to their own good. A proper functioning of society demands a high degree of consensus about the need for willing adherence to the norms of society. In the context of a discussion on population control, Rosemary Ruether makes the point that societies such as China which appear to be very coercive apparently can be perceived by the vast majority of those within them as free and liberated because of their communal elan.[13] Society thus needs a broad-based voluntary consent to its guiding norms and principles if it is to be effective.

Applied to the question of the problem of population control, this means that heavy emphasis must be given to the education and motivation of the individuals with a great respect for their freedom to responsibly choose in the light of the total needs of the society. The report of the Commission on Population Growth and the American Future warns that groups which feel deprived and discriminated against by current government policies will be skeptical and resistant to new governmental programs in the population field.[14] This does not exclude at times the possibility that coercion might be necessary, but coercion can never be the first or primary means used by the state.

Another significant aspect of the theory of the state and its functions concerns the principle of subsidiarity and its application to questions such as population control. Subsidiarity declares the larger and higher collectivities should not take over the functions which can be performed by smaller and lesser groups. In population matters, according to André Hellegers, it means that there be no unnecessary curtailment or abrogation of free, individual decision-making.[15] However, a full and accurate picture must also recognize the principle of socialization which emerged in Roman Catholic social ethics in the encyclicals of Pope John XXIII. Pope John points out that one of the principal characteristics of our modern age is an increase in social relationships. This will at times call for greater government intervention and for national and international movements, but these increased social relationships should not reduce human beings to the condition of mere automatons.[16] More so than Hellegers, Joseph Kiernan rightly points out the need to recognize both subsidiarity and socialization (solidarity-justice) in discussing population questions so that considerations of subsidiarity are not absolutized.[17] In practice this means that larger communities including the state may have to intervene in population control if this is deemed necessary.

3. *Freedom and the Right to Procreate*

One of the most important considerations concerns the freedom of the individual couple in determining family size. Some proposals for population control call for coercion as a necessary means of achieving optimum population. Through one means or another the state would control the number of children that individuals are able to procreate. The World Population Plan of Action adopted by the recent United Nations conference in Bucharest recommends that all countries respect and insure, regardless of their overall demographic goals, the rights of persons to determine in a free, informed and responsible manner the number and spacing of their children. This recommendation is in keeping with a traditional emphasis in United Nations literature on the freedom of the individual couple in questions of the size of their family.[18]

From my theological-ethical perspective, the freedom of the couple is very important. Through having children one responds to a very fundamental human desire and need. The freedom of the individual in this matter is very closely associated with human dignity and the basic core freedom of the human person. However, freedom is not the only important moral value which is to be considered here. Phrased in another way, this means that the freedom of the couple must be limited and influenced by other factors.

The older Roman Catholic teaching recognized something more than just the freedom of the individuals to do what they choose. The older Catholic teaching so stressed the aspect of the good of the species as to assert that the primary purpose of marriage and sexuality was the procreation and education of offspring, and that every single act of sexual intercourse had to be open to the possibilities of procreation.[19] The prohibition of artificial contraception rests (wrongly in my judgment) on this understanding of the fact that every act of sexual intercourse involves more than merely the couple and their freedom. The species aspect of human sexuality in the traditional Catholic approach has always had a pronatalist assumption, but logically such an emphasis could also call for a limitation of births if this was required by the needs of the human species. By stressing the primary end of marriage as the procreation and education of offspring, the traditional Roman Catholic theology also recognizes that the upbringing or education of the child is an important factor in the decision of the couple to have a child. This teaching thus recognizes that there are limits placed on couples in terms of their right to procreate offspring.

In keeping with traditional ethical terminology, one can assert that individual couples have the right to procreate offspring, but the exercise of that right is limited. In exercising their rights couples must act responsibly. If individual couples for some reason or other do not act responsibly, then if there is harm being done to the public order of society, the state can intervene to insure that individuals act in a more responsible manner. In addition there is a very important distinction between the right of the individual couple to have offspring and the right of an individual couple to have a particular number of children. It is much easier to recognize that the state can intervene in terms of restricting the number of children that a particular couple could have since this is not as basic and fundamental a right as the right to procreate children in general. However, the fact that the state can intervene must not be taken for a *carte blanche* authorization, for government coercion remains a last resort. There are many other questions that have to be settled before one could decide that the state should intervene and precisely how it should intervene.

If it is necessary for the state to intervene and curtail the freedom of individuals, then this must be done in accord with justice and other relevant moral principles.

This understanding of the right to procreate and its limitations seems preferable to describing it as a social right.[20]

4. *Proper Description of the Problem*

It is obvious that any solution to the problem of population control must be based on an adequate and objective understanding of the nature of the problem itself. Judgments in moral theology are heavily dependent on empirical data, but the division between facts and values is much more complicated than might seem at first sight. Today we are more conscious of the fact that it is very difficult if not impossible to speak about something as being objective and value-free. Very often judgments which claim to be purely objective and based on empirical data alone contain concealed value judgments about what is more important and why.[21]

In attempting a proper description and understanding of the population problem one must also honestly recognize one's own presuppositions and prejudices. As a general approach I eschew overly simplistic solutions to human ethical problems. This presupposition arises in theory from a more relational ethical model which sees the individual ethical actor in terms of multiple relationships with God, neighbor and the world. My insistence on complexity also comes from the recognition that very often erroneous solutions are proposed not because of some error of commission but because of omission—the failure to consider all the elements that must be discussed.

From my perspective I am inclined to accept the analysis of Philip Hauser that human beings are complex culture-building animals, and the population crisis is really a series of four crises or problems. First, the population explosion maintains that, assuming the present trend, by the year 2000 the population of the developing countries will be about the same or as great as the total population of the world in 1960. Second, the population implosion refers to the increasing concentration of people on relatively small portions of the earth's surface, a phenomenon generally known as urbanization. Third, the population displosion means the increasing heterogeneity of people who share the same geographical space as well as the same social, political and economic conditions and is exemplified by the current problems in Northern Ireland and many countries in Africa or even in Canada. Fourth, the technoplosion refers to the accelerated pace of technological innovation which has characterized our modern era.[22] Hauser acknowledges that in the developing countries much yet remains to be done before the control of the population explosion is assured.[23] But Hauser also asserts that it is almost certain that problems created or exacerbated by implosion and displosion will create more human misery during at least the remainder of this century than the problems produced by excessive fertility and growth.[24]

Population control cannot be limited merely to providing the means for individuals to control fertility. Under population goals and policies, the World Population Plan of Action mentions in addition to population growth the need for policies and goals in the following areas: reduction of morbidity and mortality; reproduction, family formation and the status of women; population distribution and internal migration; international migration and population structure.[25] The recommendation of the Study Committee of the Office of the Foreign Secretary of the National Academy of Sciences includes these and other considerations.[26]

Personal and national narrowness of perception as well as sinfulness may at times affect the understanding and statement of the problem as well as proposed solutions. In general the developed nations of the world tended to see the problem of population control and most of the problems of the developing nations in terms of the need to cut down on the number of births. In the eyes of the United States government before the Bucharest meeting in 1974, population growth was a problem because it has many effects including retarding economic growth and negatively affecting food resources, the environment and governmental abilities to meet these needs. Given the causal importance of population growth, massive spending on contraceptive development in family planning programs was the one major solution proposed. A more nuanced view was taken by some American scholars such as Donald Warwick[27] and Arthur Dyck,[28] a Christian ethicist from Harvard, who pointed out that problems such as environmental deterioration, starvation and poverty as they exist today are not directly and mainly caused by present population growth rates. Neuhaus and others viewed the American emphasis on contraception and family planning as an unwillingness to admit many of the problems caused by the over-consumption of the developed nations and by the inequitable economic structures of modern existence.[29] Even before the 1974 meeting in Bucharest there was a growing realization that a more integral view of the interdependent character of population and social phenomena such as social and economic change, environmental factors and technological developments was required. Population growth is not the only problem, nor the cause of all the problems, nor the major obstacle to the solution of all problems.[30]

A final caution in understanding the population problem and its solution stems from the limitations of any one science. The scientific, in general, is not totally identical with the human; also the perspective of one science can never be totally identical with the human perspective. One must critically examine various understandings and solutions because of the danger of distortion. Psychology is more interested in the individual, whereas sociology is more concerned about society. The fact that something is genetically possible does not always mean it should be done. In general one must be aware of solutions proposed in the name of only a partial perspective or from the viewpoint of only one science or optique.

Specific Proposals

Having considered four important theological-ethical considerations which inform the ethical judgment about population problems, the following specific proposals will be discussed: (1) a wholistic solution; (2) triage; (3) means used by governments to control population; (4) means of fertility and birth control; and (5) the role of the Roman Catholic Church.

1. A Wholistic Solution

Solutions for the population problem must be integral and wholistic. It is morally wrong merely to propose decreasing the number of births without recognizing the multifaceted nature of the problem which must include other demographic components and social and economic changes. There always remains the danger that the powerful and strong will be tempted to see the solution only in the realm of preventing births and lowering fertility. It is now recognized that many of the problems of the environment are caused as much by the over-consumption of the developed nations as by the birth rate in the developing nations.

There is also good evidence to support the fact that programs aimed at lowering fertility will not be successful unless they are accompanied by social and economic changes. Arthur Dyck relates in a number of articles the poignant story of the ghetto mother which was first told by Robert Coles. To poverty-stricken mothers in the ghettos of the United States a new child is a source of hope, joy and fulfillment which cannot be had in any other way. The more wealthy people in society may find their fulfillment in many other ways; but for the woman interviewed by Coles, child-bearing and raising was the one source of fulfillment in her life.[31] Many other studies indicate the same result. India's programs based only on massive contraception and sterilization have been a failure.[32]

Here it seems that good morality will have good results in practice—a point which Roman Catholic theology has often been willing to admit in the past. However, one must also point out that narrow efficiency and ethical rightness do not necessarily coincide at all times. In the question of population control, it seems that fertility control is programmatically ineffective, not feasible and politically and individually unacceptable if there is not the motivation which occurs when societies through socioeconomic development offer their members alternatives that promise an improvement in the future quality of life.[33] Thus one cannot emphasize enough the need for wholistic solutions which require not only changes in the birth rate of developing nations but changes in other demographic components, changes in the consumption of developed nations and changes in the socioeconomic structures in our world.

2. Triage

Even the more popular press has been discussing triage in the light of the population problem.[34] Triage ethics comes to the fore in disaster situations in which there is available a limited supply of medical personnel and/or services so that not all can be cared for. Decisions must be made to care for some and not for others. The hopelessly wounded and those who need greater treatment are left to die without any treatment so that treatment can be given to a greater number of others.

In 1967 William and Paul Paddock in *Famine—1975! America's Decision: Who Will Survive?* pointed to India as the bellwether of what will happen to other nations. It will be impossible to feed and help all the people in the world. The hungry nations of 1967 will become tomorrow the starving nations. Some decisions must be made about giving no further help to certain nations.[35] Garrett Hardin talked about the tragedy of the commons which shows the fundamental error of sharing ethics. In a pasture run as a commons each herdsman will tend to add more cattle because it is to one's individual benefit. Before long, the common pasture will be overcrowded and deteriorate to the detriment of all. In late 1974, Hardin continued his attack on sharing ethics by invoking the metaphor of lifeboat ethics. The rich nations of this world are comparatively well-stocked boats which are able to survive, but many poor nations with their people cannot survive. If we in the United States today take all or too many others aboard our lifeboat, it will sink. A world food bank and unrestricted immigration exemplify the tragedy of the commons. A sharing ethics will eventually destroy those who unwisely succumb to their humanitarian impulses and will only delay the day of reckoning for poor countries.[36]

Both lifeboat ethics and triage have been discussed by ethicists in the past. Edmond Cahn sees in the lifeboat situation the full force of the morals of the last day. In this situation the individual, stripped of all distinguishing features and special bonds, is left a generic creature embodying the entire genus and having no moral individuality left so that whoever kills another in that situation kills humankind. If none sacrifice themselves of free will, they must all wait and die together.[37]

Paul Ramsey argues that in the lifeboat situation random selection best assures the basic moral principle of the sanctity of the individual in deciding who can be saved and who cannot be saved.[38] Later, Ramsey admits one describable exception to the principle guaranteeing by random selection equal possibility of life when not all can be saved—if and only if a community and its members share a single focus or purpose or goal under now quite extraordinary circumstances. Ramsey gives as two examples the lifeboat situation in which some are needed because of their special expertise in rowing in order for any to be saved and in triage in disaster medicine where first priority must be given to victims who can quickly be restored to functioning. Thus even a Christian ethicist such as Paul Ramsey, who insists quite strongly on the sanctity (not just the dignity) of the individual, recognizes the moral possibility of triage and some lifeboat ethics.[39]

Although triage and some aspects of lifeboat ethics in my judgment are at times morally acceptable, they are not moral now in the question of population control because the problem, as real and as important as it is, is not now catastrophic or simply focused. We are not in the last days; there is still time for other solutions. Above all the problem is not simply a problem of fertility control but involves many other demographic, social and economic factors so that the rich nations of the world are also at fault and not just the poor nations. Hardin fails to recognize that the problem is multifaceted and not simply a problem of the poor nations producing too many offspring.

Hardin's proposals do not give the respect for the individual which a Christian understanding of the individual and of Christian love calls for. He is too willing to sacrifice many people when it is not necessary and especially when the proper moral response might call for a more generous action on our part. Not only is it a question of the dignity of the individual human being but also the interdependence of all human beings which Christianity as well as many rational ethics recognize. This interdependence is seen in the numerous ways in which rich and poor countries are related so that the problem cannot be blamed solely on any one group. The irony is that the rich nations of the world have enriched themselves precisely through an exploitation of the poor nations. Lately the energy crisis has made many Americans much more aware of the interdependence of our own human existence. Not only is triage in this situation morally wrong because it does not give enough respect for the meaning of the individual and of the demands of Christian love for those in need, but it also goes against the basic understanding of the interdependent nature of human existence today and therefore even pragmatically is impossible. No one nation or group of nations will be able to go it alone because of our mutual dependencies.

Survival itself is not an absolute or the most important human value and imperative. The moral corollary of this statement is that there are certain things we should not do even if they aid the quest for survival. As Daniel Callahan has pointed out, the need for survival is modified by the need to realize other values such as freedom, justice and a sense of dignity and worth. There are some means of assuring survival which are themselves morally wrong so that it would be better not to survive than have to survive in such a moral atmosphere.[40]

3. Means Used by Governments

How should the state deal with the problem of controlling population growth? In one of the most comprehensive and synthetic articles on the question of population control, Bernard Berelson lists and summarizes the proposals which have been advanced in the literature—extensions of voluntary fertility control, establishment of involuntary fertility control, intensified educational campaigns, incentive programs, tax and welfare benefits and penalties, shifts in social and economic institutions and political channels and organizations.[41] In my judgment the primary ethical considerations in addition to the proportionality of benefits and harms are freedom and justice, although these elements can be expanded in different ways. The Study Committee of the Office of the Foreign Secretary of the National Academy of Sciences, for example, recommends the ethical criteria for fertility control policies which were first proposed in the above-cited article by Berelson.[42]

As mentioned earlier, freedom is a most important value but cannot be absolutized. On a scale of government interference in a continuum from freedom to coercive policies, the following general approaches can be identified: education, motivation and propaganda for population control together with provision of acceptable means to control fertility to all who want and need them; change of social structures which affect demography; incentives offered to control population; and coercive methods employed by the government.

Questions of justice arise especially in considerations of incentives and coercion. Robert Veatch elaborates eight criteria which should be used in judging incentive proposals, but he recognizes that the principle of justice creates the gravest difficulty for incentive proposals. The ultimate reasons from justice raised against incentive proposals stem from discrimination. Discrimination exists often toward the poor who are most tempted by monetary inducements and subject to abuse in the process, whereas the wealthy are not put under that same pressure. Likewise, incentives can harm innocent children if certain penalties or lack of services are provided for the nth child born in each family.[43] Veatch proposes as a just incentive a progressive sliding-scale fee which might be called a child welfare fee payable every year for every child.[44] Dyck accepts as the least unjust of all incentive programs the provision of pensions for poor parents with fewer than n children, as a social security for their old age which takes away the insecurity which in some societies is met by the children.[45] Edward Pohlman argues that incentives are not ideal but they are necessary today.[46] In somewhat the same manner Melvin Ketchel says that compulsory fertility control would seem to be the most effective and the least objectionable of any involuntary methods.[47]

In judging the morality of government policy one must again insist on a wholistic perspective. Fertility control is not acceptable if it is the only solution because it is necessary also to see the problem in the context of other demographic, economic and social factors. All the lower efforts on the scale from freedom to incentives and coercion must be employed first before one can even think about incentives and coercion. There is an intense need for education, motivation and the provision of morally acceptable means of fertility control to all who want them as well as the need for changing social structures (e.g., the status of women) which affect demography. At the present time except in extraordinary circumstances, it does not seem that coercion is acceptable. In some situations incentives might be morally acceptable, but here special care should be taken lest fundamental principles of justice are violated. Although perfect justice is never attainable, special concern for the rights of the poor is needed. In addition, the very important pragmatic note should be made that if incentives are employed without all the other means mentioned above, they will apparently be ineffective.

The problem of freedom and coercion does not exist only where there is an attempt by government to cut down the size of populations. There are some countries in the world today (e.g., Brazil and Argentina), which are trying to increase their population; but here, too, the same moral question arises about the means employed by the government to bring about the desired population.[48] The freedom of couples and their right to determine the number of children they want should be protected. The government has the obligation of allowing couples to plan their families and of supplying the poor with the acceptable means they need to be able to achieve the legitimate goals of family planning. Here again the distinction between family planning and population control is significant. In the name of population control the government cannot take away from individuals the right to plan and limit their own families in accord with their understanding of what is right and helpful. However, the government can through education and motivation show the need for an increase in population and appeal to the generosity of families to carry this out.

4. *Means of Fertility and Birth Control*

Contraception, sterilization and abortion are the principal means which individuals use to prevent conception and birth. What about the morality of these means? From the viewpoint of morality there is general acceptance in the world of the morality of artificial contraception. The official teaching of the hierarchical magisterium of the Roman Catholic Church condemns artificial contraception, but dissent from such official teaching is, in my judgment, both justifiable and widespread in Roman Catholicism.[49] Sterilization from an ethical viewpoint is logically viewed in the same moral category as contraception with the significant difference that sterilization tends to be permanent. The official hierarchical teaching of the Roman Catholic Church continues to condemn all direct sterilization, but as noted in the preceding chapter there is in my judgment justifiable and growing dissent from such teaching.[50] The primary ethical problems connected with contraception and sterilization come from government policies involving incentives or coercion, but these have already been discussed.

Abortion as a means of preventing births and as an instrument of population control raises many more serious ethical problems and objections. The World Population Plan of Action accepted at Bucharest shows the tension existing within the world community on the question of abortion. In considering morbidity and mortality the document recommends the reduction of illegal abortions.[51] Proposed amendments to change "illegal" to "induced" and to replace "abortion" with "miscarriage" were both defeated.[52] The Report of the Commission on Population Growth and the American Future made the following recommendation: "Therefore with the admonition that abortion not be considered a primary means of fertility control, the Commission recommends that present state laws restricting abortion be abriged along the lines of the New York State statute. . . ."[53] The Study Committee of the Office of the Foreign Secretary of the National Academy of Sciences recommended that legal and social barriers to fertility control be promptly removed and broad social acceptance and support of fertility control including medically safe abortions should be fostered.[54]

The Commission on Population Growth and the American Future recognized that at the present time it is difficult to make precise quantitative statements concerning the demographic import of abortion.[55] Arthur Dyck, while reporting that permissive abortion generally facilitates a downward trend in population and that restrictive abortion policies do not prevent a downward trend in fertility, concludes that abortion is not needed to solve population problems.[56] Abdel R. Omran maintains that when developing countries are highly motivated to accelerate their transition from high to low fertility induced abortion becomes a popular method of fertility control. Omran concludes his study by emphasizing two major themes for policy formation: (1) there is no question that prevention of pregnancy through effective contraception is much wiser and safer than the termination of pregnancy through abortion;

(2) for reasons that vary from country to country, a margin of induced abortion is to be anticipated and provided for.[57] The primary ethical question is not whether or not abortion is an effective means of population control, although it does seem from the evidence mentioned above that Dyck is correct in asserting that abortion is not necessary as a means of population control.[58]

Opposition to abortion on ethical grounds cannot be based merely on its efficacy or inefficacy in terms of population control. It must be pointed out that opposition to abortion on ethical grounds is not limited to Roman Catholicism, as is exemplified in Arthur Dyck's writings. Elsewhere I have discussed the morality of abortion and concluded that individual human life is present between the fourteenth and the twenty-first day after conception, and only the life of the mother or a value commensurate with life morally justifies abortion after that time.[59] The next chapter will discuss the question of abortion laws and reactions to the decision of the Supreme Court about abortion. However, my acceptance of some legal abortions does not mean that I accept abortion as a means of population control to be proposed and promoted by the government. Active promotion of abortion by governments as a means of population control in my judgment is both morally wrong and not necessary. Above all, compulsory abortion is an ethical monstrosity that cannot be accepted.

5. The Role of the Roman Catholic Church

There is no doubt that the Roman Catholic teaching condemning artificial contraception puts the Catholic Church in a difficult posture in terms of population control.[60] I have strongly dissented from such teaching and have urged that it be changed, but unfortunately from a realistic perspective I do not think that the official teaching will be changed in the very near future. In the meantime it seems that many Catholic couples and clergy will continue to dissent so that in pastoral practice most Catholics do not seem to have a problem with the use of artificial contraception. Despite the existing teaching, there is thus a way around the problem in pastoral practice for individual Catholic couples. However, the present official teaching of the Roman Catholic Church continues to condemn artificial contraception as a means of family planning and population control.

Even though I personally go much further, there is a better position that can be taken by the official teaching of the Roman Catholic Church. Couples in a pluralistic society have the right to choose the means (not abortion) by which they will plan their families and respond to the need for population control, and the government can provide them with the help necessary to carry out their decision. Such an approach is both in conformity with developing Catholic teaching on freedom in a pluralistic society as developed in the preceding chapter, and is better than mere opposition to family planning and population control. From the perspective of the official Roman Catholic teaching, one must also insist that the government provide help in the rhythm method for those who choose to use natural family planning.

There are two interesting anomalies about the present official position of the Roman Catholic Church. First, without the acceptance and provision of artificial contraception there is evidence that in developing countries many people during a transitional period revert to abortion.[61] Second, John Hayes, an Irish Catholic social ethician, has pointed out that by fostering economic development through its social teachings the Roman Catholic Church is also promoting a situation in which the data show that contraceptive practices become more widespread.[62]

It is imperative for official Catholic Church teaching to recognize the existence and gravity of the population problem. In *Populorum Progressio* in 1967, Pope Paul did acknowledge to some degree the existence of the problem,[63] but ever since that time there have been many occasions, both official and unofficial, in which the problem was ignored or downplayed. In an address to the World Food Congress in Rome in November 1974, Pope Paul did not recognize the existence of a population problem and the need for population control.[64] The November 1973 statement of the National Conference of Catholic Bishops of the United States is to be applauded, for the American bishops called on Catholic people to take a positive approach to the question of population.[65] Fortunately, Catholic scholars in the United States and abroad have been taking such approaches. Official Roman Catholic teaching must recognize the existence of the problem and urge governments and people to take steps necessary to deal with it, for the problem is only to become more acute in the years ahead. However, the official Church teaching must also help to situate this problem in a broader perspective involving the sharing of food and resources and economic development (as Catholic statements have often done), and must insist on the many ethical values which necessarily enter into the discussion, especially considerations of freedom and justice involving the rights of the poor and innocent.

NOTES

1. Bernard Berelson, "Beyond Family Planning," *Science* 163 (1969): 533–543; Kingsley Davis, "Population Policy: Will Current Problems Succeed?" *Science* 158 (1967): 730–739; Arthur McCormack, "The Population Explosion: A Theologian's Concern?" *Theological Studies* 35 (1974): 3–19.

2. United Nations Economic and Social Council, "World Population Plan of Action," *World Population Conference* (October 2, 1974) E/5585, par. n. 3.

3. Martin C. D'Arcy, *The Mind and Heart of Love* (New York: Meridian Books, 1956); Jules Toner, *The Experience of Love* (Washington, D.C.: Corpus Books, 1968).

4. Pope John XXIII, *Pacem in Terris* (New York: Paulist Press, 1963). The original is found in *Acta Apostolicae Sedis* 55 (1963): 257–304.

5. Michael J. Walsh, "The Holy See's Population Problem," *The Month* 7 (1974): 632–636; Francis X. Murphy, "The Pope and our Common Future," *Worldview* 18 (February 1975): 23–28.

6. Pope Paul VI, *On the Development of Peoples (Populorum Progressio)* (New York: Paulist Press, 1967). The original is found in *Acta Apostolicae Sedis* 59 (1967): 257–289.

7. Pope Paul VI, "Address to the World Food Congress, Nov. 9. 1974," *The Pope Speaks* 19 (1975): 208–215. The original is found in *Acta Apostolicae Sedis* 66 (1974): 644–652.

8. Helmut Thielicke, *Theological Ethics*, vol. 2: *Politics* (Philadelphia: Fortress Press, 1969).

9. R. A. Markus, "Two Conceptions of Political Authority: Augustine, *De Civitate Dei* XIX, 14–15, and some Thirteenth-century Interpretations," *The Journal of Theological Studies* 16 (1965): 69–100; Heinrich Rommen, *The State in Catholic Thought* (St. Louis: B. Herder, 1945).

10. Eric D'Arcy, *Conscience and Its Right to Freedom* (New York: Sheed and Ward, 1961).

11. Pius Augustine, *Religious Freedom in Church and State* (Baltimore: Helicon, 1966).

12. John Courtney Murray, *The Problem of Religious Freedom* (Westminster, Md.: Newman Press, 1965).

13. Rosemary Radford Ruether, "Governmental Coercion and One-Dimensional Thinking," in *The Population Crisis and Moral Responsibility*, ed. J. Philip Wogaman (Washington: Public Affairs Press, 1973), pp. 167–173.

14. "Report of the Commission on Population Growth and The

American Future," *Population and the American Future* (New York: New American Library, 1972), p. 91.

15. André E. Hellegers, "Government Planning and the Principle of Subsidiarity," in *The Population Crisis and Moral Responsibility,* pp. 137–144.

16. Pope John XXIII, *Mater et Magistra* (New York: Paulist Press, 1961), n. 59–66. The original is found in *Acta Apostolicae Sedis* 53 (1961): 401–464.

17. Joseph Kiernan, "An Analysis of Certain Population Policies," *The American Ecclesiastical Review* 169 (1975): 118–132.

18. *World Population Conference,* par. n. 13.

19. John C. Ford and Gerald Kelly, *Contemporary Moral Theology,* vol. 2: *Marriage Questions* (Westminster, Md.: Newman Press, 1963).

20. Yale Task Force on Population Ethics, "Moral Claims, Human Rights, and Population Policies," *Theological Studies* 35 (1974): 105.

21. Daniel Callahan, "Introduction," in *The American Population Debate,* ed. Daniel Callahan (New York: Doubleday, 1971), p. xii; Stanley Hauerwas, "The Moral Limits of Population Control," *Thought* 49 (1974): 240.

22. Philip M. Hauser, "Population Criteria in Foreign Aid Programs," in *The Population Crisis and Moral Responsibility,* pp. 233–239.

23. Philip M. Hauser, "World Population: Retrospect and Prospect," in *Rapid Population Growth* (Baltimore and London: The Johns Hopkins University Press, 1971), p. 121.

24. Hauser, *Population Crisis and Moral Responsibility,* p. 236.

25. *World Population Conference,* par. nn. 20–67.

26. Study Commission of the Office of the Foreign Secretary, National Academy of Sciences, *Rapid Population Growth* (Baltimore and London: Johns Hopkins University Press, 1971), pp. 77–89.

27. Donald P. Warwick, "Ethics and Population Control in Developing Countries," *The Hastings' Center Report* 4 (June 1974): 1.

28. Arthur J. Dyck, "Is Abortion Necessary to Solve Population Problems?" in *Abortion and Social Ethics,* ed. T. Hilgers and D. Horan (New York: Sheed and Ward, 1972), p. 164.

29. Richard John Neuhaus, *In Defense of People: Ecology and the Seduction of Radicalism* (New York: Macmillan, 1971).

30. Peter J. Henriot, "Global Population in Perspective: Implications for U.S. Policy Response," *Theological Studies* 35 (1974): 50.

31. Arthur J. Dyck, "Population Policies and Ethical Acceptability," in *Rapid Population Growth,* p. 633; "Procreative Rights and Population Policies," *The Hasting's Center Studies* 1 (1973): 75–76; "American Global Population Policy: An Ethical Analysis." *Linacre Quarterly* 42 (1975): 60.

32. John F. X. Harriott, "Bucharest and Beyond," *The Month* 7 (1974): 630.

33. Henriot, *Theological Studies* 35 (1974): 58.

34. E.g., Wade Greene, "Triage," *The New York Times Magazine,* December 5, 1975.

35. William and Paul Paddock, *Famine—1975! America's Decision: Who Will Survive?* (New York: Little, Brown and Co., 1967).

36. Garrett Hardin, "The Tragedy of the Commons," *Science* 162 (1968): 1243–1248; "Living on a Lifeboat," *Bioscience* 24 (1974): 561–568.

37. Edmond Cahn, *The Moral Decision* (Bloomington and London: Indiana University Press, 1955), pp. 61–71.

38. Paul Ramsey, *Nine Modern Moralists* (Englewood Cliffs, N.J.: Prentice Hall, 1962), p. 245.

39. Paul Ramsey, *The Patient as Person* (New Haven and London: Yale University Press, 1970), pp. 257–259.

40. Daniel Callahan, "Population and Human Survival," in *The Population Crisis and Moral Responsibility,* pp. 58–59; "Doing Well by Doing Good," *The Hastings Center Report* 4 (December 1974): 1–4.

41. Berelson, "Beyond Family Planning," *Science* 163 (1969): 533–543.

42. *Rapid Population Growth,* p. 81.

43. Robert M. Veatch, "Governmental Incentives: Ethical Issues at Stake," in *The Population Crisis and Moral Responsibility,* pp. 207–224.

44. Ibid., p. 220.

45. Dyck, "Population Policies and Ethical Acceptability," in *Rapid Population Growth,* p. 622.

46. Edward Pohlman, *Incentives and Compensations in Birth Planning,* Carolina Population Center Monograph 11 (1971).

47. Melvin Ketchel, "Fertility Control Agents as a Possible Solution to the World Population Problem," in *The American Population Debate,* p. 295.

48. Warwick, *Hastings Center Report* 4, (June 1974): 1–4.

49. Frederick E. Crowe, "The Conscience of the Theologian with Reference to the Encyclical," in *Conscience: Its Freedom and Limitations,* ed. William C. Bier (New York: Fordham University Press, 1971) pp. 312–332.

50. Charles E. Curran, "Sterilization: Roman Catholic Theory and Practice," *New Perspectives in Moral Theology* (Notre Dame, Ind.: University of Notre Dame Press, 1976), pp. 194–211.

51. *World Population Conference,* par. n. 246.

52. Ibid., par. n. 137.

53. *Population and the American Future,* p. 178.

54. *Rapid Population Growth,* p. 84.

55. *Population and the American Future,* p. 176.

56. Dyck, *Abortion and Social Justice,* pp. 166–168.

57. Abdel R. Omran, "Abortion and Demographic Transition," in *Rapid Population Growth*, pp. 479–532.

58. Dyck, *Abortion and Social Justice*, p. 165.

59. Curran, *New Perspectives in Moral Theology*, pp. 163–193.

60. Denis E. Hurley, "Population Control and the Catholic Conscience: Responsibility of the Magisterium," *Theological Studies* 35 (1974): 154–163.

61. Omran, *Rapid Population Growth*, pp. 486ff.

62. John Hayes, "Aspects of the World Population Problem," *Social Studies* 3 (1974): 243.

63. *Populorum Progressio*, par. n. 37.

64. Walsh, *The Month* 7 (1974): 632–636; Murphy, *Worldview* 18 (Feb., 1975): 23–28.

65. National Conference of Catholic Bishops, "Statement on Population," *Origins* 3 (November 29, 1973): 353ff.

8: Respect for Life: Theoretical and Practical Implications

Respect for life is a phrase that is frequently heard in our society today. Not only is it a very important concept, but its implications and extensions are manifold. Any adequate analysis of respect for life should include at least three important aspects of the question: (1) the basis and reasons for respect for life; (2) the implications or applications to various areas or aspects of life; (3) the strategies or ways of trying to implement and even institutionalize in society the respect for life. It is impossible to cover adequately and completely all these aspects. Since the areas of life to which it is applied include many significant issues—abortion, capital punishment, war, the elderly, the poor, the hungry, the sick, the institutionalized, the oppressed, the retarded—prudence dictates that only a few implications or applications can be made in the second part of this study.

I. The Basis of Respect for Life

The question can be stated simply: Whence comes the dignity, the sanctity or the respect due to human life? The answer generally accepted in the Christian community is from the special relation of the human being to the life-giving act of God and from the destiny of each person. Creation of the individual, who is destined by a loving God for the fullness of life, constitutes the basis, although not the total explanation, of the dignity and respect for human life.[1]

Catholic theological ethics has highlighted creation as the basic reason for the dignity and sanctity of human life because an appeal was often made in Catholic thought not only to revelation but also to reason and natural law. On the basis of reason, according to what had been an accepted Catholic position, one can come to the recognition of the fact of creation. All should acknowledge that human life comes from God and human persons do not have full dominion over their lives.[2] Also other natural law arguments, prescinding from revelation but emphasizing the uniqueness of the human, have been proposed as the basis for the dignity of and respect for human life.[3] One example of this reasoning acknowledged by all (as often pointed out by Catholic authors) can be found in the International Declaration of Rights proposed by the General Assembly of the United Nations in 1948.[4] Catholic thought thus recognizes that one does not have to be a believer to affirm the dignity of human life.

The simple but profound Christian insight that the dignity of, sanctity of, and respect for human life come from the fact of creation and the resultant destiny to the fullness of life runs counter to many commonly accepted notions in our society. In the eyes of many, personal dignity and respect depend on what one does, makes or accomplishes. It is not who we are, but what we do, that is of primary importance. How easily success or accomplishments can become the basis of dignity and respect for human life. All of us are guilty of treating important people much differently from ordinary

people. Look at the way in which governmental structures and people in the structure treat the poor on welfare compared with the dignified and even red-carpet
treatment which academics or researchers who are applying for huge government grants often receive. How
often our everyday conversation indicates that the primary question concerns what a person does and not who
a person is!

Our work-conscious and pelagian mentality only
tends to exaggerate the role of works, success and accomplishments as the basis for the respect and dignity
accorded to the human person. That is why there is a
tendency to forget about the elderly, the retarded, the
poor, the sick and the institutionalized. If individuals
are not contributing members of society, then all too
easily they can be written off. Here the difference that
comes from varying views on the basis for the dignity
and respect for human life becomes evident. How does
a society treat the oppressed, the poor and the weak?

The basic Christian approach steming from creation
is strengthened by the further Christian emphasis on
revelation, redemption and Christian love. God's way of
dealing with us as illustrated in his choice of the poor,
the sinner and the children as the privileged people in
the kingdom of God shows again that ultimate value
comes from God's gracious gift to us. This gift-giving
love of God then becomes normative for the Christian,
so that our love for the neighbor must be modeled at
least in some way on God's love for us. Hence the poor,
the weak, the needy and the oppressed have always oc-
cupied an important place in the language and rhetoric,
if not in the practice, of Christian love. In fact, the
Christian is truly biased and prejudiced in favor of the
needy and weak.

The tradition of Catholic moral theology cautions us

to recognize some of the nuances and complexities involved in determining precisely how one understands this gift of life as being found in and accepted by the individual person. In this connection there is a danger in so stressing the aspect of life as gift that the role and place of the human response is downplayed. The Catholic tradition, generally speaking in contrast to a large part of the Protestant tradition, has insisted on the human response and even human works. This is very clear in the theological controversy over justification and sanctification or the role of faith and works in the life of a Christian, but it is also true in the case of our understanding of the human. Thomas Aquinas maintains that the human being is an image of God precisely insofar as one is endowed with intellect and will and has dominion over one's activity. Thus the human person becomes an image of God precisely in and through self-determination.[5] The very fact of receiving life as a gift of God is not all that can or should be said about the full dignity of the human person.

Take, now, a very significant practical example of a nuanced understanding of creation as the basis of human dignity. If one were to see life only as a gift and the individual with no power or stewardship whatsoever, then one would conclude that the individual must do everything possible to keep human life in existence. Some thinkers in the Protestant tradition have argued this way.[6] But the Catholic tradition has generally acknowledged that our stewardship is to be exercised in a reasonable way, so that one does not have to do everything possible to keep human life in existence. In the Catholic tradition there arose the principle that no one is obliged to use extraordinary means to preserve human life in existence. Extraordinary means have been defined as those means not commonly used in given circumstances, or those means in common use which this individual in one's present physical, psychological or economic condition cannot reasonably employ or, if employed, will not give a definite hope of proportionate benefit. The casuistry involved in understanding and applying this principle is most interesting. If a particular procedure or operation is too painful or too expensive or would cause us to be away from family and hearth for an inordinately long time, there is no obligation to use it.[7] In its own way the tradition acknowledges the quality of life arguments based on human happiness or other factors influencing what must be done to keep life in existence. The dignity of human life based on creation and gift does not exclude a stewardship that considers other values or realities in making decisions about keeping human life in existence. Thus the Catholic tradition has accepted both the notion of dignity and respect for human life, based on the fact that life is a gift from God and destined for the fullness of life, and the realization that human stewardship leaves some significant determinations in human hands.

II. Implications and Applications

One introductory point deserves to be underscored. Although an acknowledgment of the fundamental importance of respect for life does not mean that normative judgments can never permit killing, still, respect for life must have some influence and significance in the norms and judgments proposed. A credible witness of the respect for life on the part of individuals and especially on the part of the Church must apply this respect for life to all areas. Internal consistency and external credibility suffer when all the ramifications of respect for life are not acknowledged.[8]

As indicated earlier, it is impossible in this study to consider all the implications and applications of the principle of respect for life. In this section some general remarks will be followed by examining the respect for human life as it has influenced two specific questions in the Catholic tradition: abortion and the universal destiny of the goods of creation for all human beings.

It is necessary to distinguish carefully between the theoretical basis for the respect for human life and the normative question of the criteria or judgments made about human life. Christians have accepted the same general basis for the respect for human life, but differed about many questions such as capital punishment. On the other hand, Christians often find themselves in practical agreement with others who might not explicitly acknowledge creation as the basis for the dignity of human life.

In moving from the respect for human life to normative criteria and judgments there are many other factors that enter into the discussion. The Catholic and Christian traditions have not always seen war or killing in self-defense or capital punishment as opposed to and irreconcilable with respect for life. At the very least this indicates the need to recognize that one cannot naively appeal only to respect for life in determining normative moral criteria or judgments involving human life. Other elements such as conflicting claims will also come into consideration.

The prohibitions of murder and direct abortion flow from this basic understanding of the respect for life. In the case of abortion, note that the concept of dignity, sanctity or respect for life based primarily on creation and not on what one does, makes or accomplishes has played a very significant role. Even in the womb the fetus is considered a human being with all the dignity and respect of human life, for such dignity depends primarily on God's gracious gift. The question of abortion seems to illustrate quite well the differences that can emerge when there are differing views of the basis for the dignity of human life. Just because the fetus is not seen, or because it produces nothing or contributes nothing to society does not mean that it has less dignity or value than other human beings. In the light of what has been said about some aspects of our contemporary ethos, it follows that today the dignity and respect for the fetus can readily be forgotten.

However, in the abortion question the Catholic tradition has also recognized some important nuances. At times conflict situations can arise, and abortion is permitted in Catholic teaching. The strict ethical statement is that direct abortion is always wrong, but indirect abortion can be allowed for a proportionate reason. In my judgment the principle of double effect does not adequately solve the conflict situations arising in abortion. In its place I have proposed that abortion is justified to save the life of the mother or for a value commensurate with life.[9] One can disagree over the way to solve conflict situations without denying creation as the basis for the respect owed to human life.

In the Catholic tradition there has been theoretical debate and disagreement about the significant question of when human life begins. (Here and in subsequent usage 'human life' refers to truly human life, or that human life which constitutes one a being with all the rights of a human person. Some other authors distinguish between human life which might be present from the time of conception and truly, fully, or personal human life, which does not begin until later.) In practice it has been admitted that one must act as if human life is present from the very moment of conception. Why has there been some discussion about the question of the beginning of human life? The ultimate reason rests on the fact that Catholic theology and philosophy accept the principle of mediation. In attempting to discover how human beings should act morally, for example, appeal is not made directly and immediately to the will of God but rather to the nature of human beings. The plan and design of God is known mediately in and through the human. In the particular question of when human life begins, appeal is not made directly and immediately to the creative act of God but rather to that reality in the creature which indicates the presence of human life. God's gift of human life truly creates and brings about a human being. Some claim that Thomas Aquinas maintained a theory of delayed animation because he believed the organization required for a human being (the matter must be disposed to receive a human soul) was not present at the moment of conception.[10] Even those who hold in theory that human life is present from the very first moment of conception argue on the basis of the fertilized ovum and what it is, finding strong supporting evidence in the conclusions of modern biology indicating that from the moment of conception the unique genetic package of this individual human being is already present.[11]

No Roman Catholic would argue as Paul Ramsey does that from the Christian perspective the sanctity of life is not based on something inherent in the human being but on an alien dignity, because of which (from an authentic religious point of view) none of these distinctions and theories about when germinating life becomes human are important.[12] The traditional Catholic approach, which sees that the gift and the plan of God are mediated in and through the creature—and in this case the human being—argues differently. It is very illuminating that someone like Aquinas and others in the Catholic tradition could accept the respect for life based on creation and still argue for a later beginning of human life. At the very least, one can conclude that upholding respect for life and even its basis in creation is not incompatible with maintaining that a human being is not present from the moment of conception.

Another implication of the dignity of and respect for life based on creation and God's gift concerns the fundamental understanding about the common destiny of the goods of creation. The Catholic tradition holds that the lower forms of creation are meant to serve the higher. This basic ordering has been specified further in terms of the universal or common purpose of created things. The Pastoral Constitution on the Church in the Modern World maintains that God intended the earth and all that it contains for the use of every human being. On this basis, the document affirms that the right to have a share of earthly goods sufficient for oneself and one's family belongs to everyone (par. n. 69). Pope Paul VI asserts in *Populorum Progressio* that all other rights whatsoever, including that of private property and of free commerce, are to be subordinated to this principle (par. n. 22). God the creator intends that the goods of creation exist for all human beings.

Here again there are some attitudes in our present ethos and culture that work against this basic implication of the meaning of respect for life based on creation. The emphasis on individualism, acquisitiveness and consumerism in our society all seem to work against the basic understanding that the goods of creation are destined for all human beings. People seem to accumulate wealth and power for themselves without any thought of others. The consciousness of many modern Americans does not seem to include the realization that the goods of creation are destined for all. This certainly seems to be true in our attitude toward the poor. Likewise, the present ecological crisis reminds us that our narrow and selfish use of the goods of creation gives no concern to other existing human beings or to those who will come after us.

The universal destiny of the goods of creation for all human beings is an implication of the respect for life based on creation. However, in applying this and working out various moral norms and judgments, it is obvious that other considerations will also come into play. Nevertheless, it seems that too often Christians have forgotten how important and central should be the understanding of the common destiny of the goods of creation. We will now consider three illustrations in the Catholic tradition of the implications of the common destiny of the goods of creation.

First, there was a fascinating development in the twelfth and thirteenth centuries about the meaning and understanding of justice which unfortunately is no longer remembered today. The *Sentences* of Peter Lombard was the textbook of philosophy and theology for the Middle Ages, and subsequent scholars taught and wrote by commenting on the *Sentences.* In the third book of *Sentences,* Peter Lombard explained his teaching about the four cardinal virtues. He defined justice in the words of Augustine—"justitia est in subveniendo miseris" (justice is in coming to the assistance of the poor).[13] In *De Trinitate,* Book 14, St. Augustine had employed this description of an act of earthly justice as distinguished from an act of eternal justice. But Peter Lombard now employs this as a definition of the cardinal virtue of justice and does not distinguish it from any other kind of justice. Why Peter Lombard chose this definition is practically an impossible question to answer, but there is clear evidence that he knew and even at times used other descriptions and definitions of justice.[14]

The later commentators on the *Sentences* then had to understand and explain or even deny that justice is defined as coming to the assistance of the poor. Many commentators before Aquinas, perhaps because of the authority of Peter Lombard and Augustine, did not hesitate in some way to accept the definition of Peter Lombard as applying Augustine's original words to justice as distinct from mercy. According to some, the difference comes from the motive—if the giving is done out of compassion, the act of giving to the poor is mercy. If giving to the poor is done because it is due the other person, the act is justice. Other commentators insist on an objective basis for the distinction between justice and mercy. To give what is necessary for oneself is mercy; to give what is superfluous is justice. Thus some of the commentators before Aquinas recognized in an objective sense that to give to the poor what is not necessary for oneself is a matter of justice. However, these authors do not speak about the obligation in justice in terms of the common good or what we would call today legal justice, nor do they refer to this as commutative justice which would demand restitution.[15]

Thomas Aquinas himself does not accept Peter Lombard's definition of justice. He knows the text from Augustine which Peter Lombard uses as a definition of justice but understands such giving as belonging directly to mercy or liberality—which is a part of justice—but not directly to justice. Aquinas does not specifically treat the question of the nature of the obligation to give what is superfluous to the poor. Some contemporary commentators hold against the generally accepted opinion, that it is in keeping with the whole of Thomistic teaching to maintain that there is an obligation in justice and not only in charity to give one's superfluous goods to the poor.[16]

As time went on, the teaching of Peter Lombard and his commentators before Aquinas was generally lost. One can summarize the later teaching in the words of Pope Leo XIII in the encyclical *Rerum Novarum*. When what necessity demands has been supplied, and one's state in life provided for, it becomes a duty to give to the indigent out of what remains over. It is a duty, not of justice (save in extreme cases), but of Christian charity—a duty not enforced by human law.[17]

One can only speculate why the teaching of the *Sentences* and the commentators was generally lost in subsequent theology. The influence of Thomas Aquinas in not accepting Peter Lombard's definition was most powerful. The acceptance of an Aristotelian concept of justice as giving another one's due also militated against Peter Lombard's definition. Casuistry about obligations of restitution and the rights of the owner in strict justice also favor seeing the obligation to give of one's superfluous goods to the poor in terms of mercy or charity and not justice. In any case, the recognition of any obligation to give to the poor rests on the respect due the human person and the destiny of the goods of creation to serve all. This historical excursus illustrates how seriously this obligation was taken by Peter Lombard and his commentators.

A second illustration of an implication of the respect for human life based on God's creation and on the destiny of the goods of creation for all comes from the Catholic teaching on a living wage. John A. Ryan, the most outstanding American Catholic social ethicist in the first half of the twentieth century, wrote as his doctoral dissertation the authoritative work entitled *A Living Wage*.[18] Ryan refutes a number of unacceptable theories of wage justice: the prevailing rate theory; exchange and equivalence theories such as the rule of equal gains, the rule of free contract or the rule of market value; and also theories based on productivity. He recognizes that the needs (not the merits) of the person constitute the partial but not complete basis for the theory of a just wage. Ryan develops three fundamental principles in arguing for the right of all workers to a living wage. The first is that God created the earth for the sustenance of *all* his children; therefore, all persons are equal in their inherent claims on the bounty of nature. The second fundamental principle is that the inherent right of access to the earth is conditioned upon and becomes actually valid through the expenditure of useful labor. Third, those who are in present control of the apportionment of the earth are obliged to permit reasonable access to these opportunities by persons who are willing to work. Therefore, everyone who is willing to work has a right in justice to sustenance from the earth on reasonable terms. Since labor is the only way for an individual to obtain a share of the goods of creation, the wages paid should be sufficient to maintain the worker in frugal comfort, since the goods of creation exist primarily for all.[19] Note that Ryan does not make need the only criterion, but it is an important one. The same emphasis on need and the universal destiny of the goods of creation furnishes the basis for asserting today that fundamental medical care should be given to all people in our society.[20]

A third illustration of the implications of the dignity of the human person and the common destiny of the goods of creation for all human beings concerns the question of private property. A study of the historical development of the authoritative papal magisterium shows two significant developments in the teaching on private property from the time of Pope Leo XIII to the present, both of which indicate the growing emphasis on the dignity of the human person and the person's right to share in the goods of creation.[21] The first development is the emphasis on the common destiny of the goods of creation and the discussion of private property within that context. In *Rerum Novarum,* Pope Leo XIII discusses private property as a natural right of human beings and as the proper solution to the dignity of the worker as distinguished from the false solution of socialism.[22] In *Populorum Progressio,* Pope Paul VI considers the whole question of private property in the light of the common destiny of the goods of creation for all human beings. In this context he condemns a type of capitalism which considers material gain the key motive for economic progress, competition as the supreme law of economics and private ownership of the means of production as an absolute right that has no limits and carries no corresponding social obligations. According to Pope Paul, one cannot condemn such abuses too strongly because the economy should be at the service of all.[23]

A second development is also most illuminating. The discussions of Thomas Aquinas and Pope Leo XIII differ in their approach to the question of private property. Aquinas in the II^a II^{ae} of the *Summa Theologica,* question 66, asks in article 1, if the possession of external things is natural for human beings. He responds affirmatively that human beings do have a natural dominion with regard to the use of things. Human beings through intellect and will order external things to themselves as an end. All other realities in creation are ordered to the finality and good of human beings. Genesis proves that human beings have this dominion. Note, however, that Thomas is here talking about a very generic possession of external things and does not discuss the precise or specific way in which this generic right is to be organized. Only in the second article does Thomas discuss the more specific question of the precise social organization of the right of individuals to possess something as their own in the sense of procuring and dispensing it on their own. Thomas acknowledges such a right to possession, but he bases it not on human nature but primarily on human sinfulness—because things would not be well taken care of if they did not have an owner and because of the goods of order and of peace in society. Aquinas quickly adds that this right of procuring and dispensing things as one's own is limited by the use of property which has a common destination.

In *Rerum Novarum* (par. nn. 5–13) Pope Leo establishes private property in the more strict sense on the basis of the argument that Thomas proposed for the more generic and basic dominion—human beings as rational creatures must provide for themselves and their families both now and in the future. However, the later documents, especially The Pastoral Constitution on the Church in the Modern World (par. nn. 69–71) and *Populorum Progressio* (par. nn. 23–24), revert more to the Thomistic approach and thus relativize and limit the right to private property in the strict sense more than Pope Leo did. This relativization and limitation of the right to private property in the strict sense and the insistence that it should always serve a social function follow from the respect for life based on creation and the universal destiny of the goods of creation.[24]

This section has discussed some implications and applications of the respect for life based on creation. There are some attitudes in our society working against this basic understanding as was pointed out in the two cases considered, but also it is necessary to nuance this respect for life in the light of many other factors.

III. Strategies for Implementing the Respect for Life

The third consideration involves the means for making the respect for life and its implications more present in our society. Here I would argue for a multiplicity of approaches and object only to those strategies that try to exclude and unnecessarily downplay other emphases. There are at least four important ways for us as a Church, as groups within the Church and as individual Christians and people to make the meaning and implications of respect for life more present in our society.

First, the need to change hearts. Christian personalism rightly stresses the fundamental importance of the need to change the hearts of individuals if any ultimate change is to be accomplished. Selfishness, individualism and lack of loving concern militate against the proper dignity of and respect for human life. Above all the Church with its emphasis on the Gospel and the call to conversion can never forget the need to change the hearts of individuals.[25]

Second, education. Education alone is never enough, for the problems are deeper than mere ignorance; but education about the respect for life and its implications forms an absolutely necessary part of any total approach in making respect for life more significant in our lives and in our society. Education should be understood in the broadest sense of the term to include, for example, the educational aspects of the witness made by individual Christians and by the Church as seen in its service of the poor, the oppressed and the unborn.

Third, care, concern and love for the individual whose dignity is often threatened in our society constitute a very important way of carrying out respect for life. On this score the record of the Church has often been admirable with its establishment of hospitals, orphanages and homes for the poor and elderly. By itself this approach would never be enough, but nonetheless there is always room for the care of the forgotten or victimized individual as part of a comprehensive approach to making respect for life more a part of the fabric of our society.

Fourth, it is not just enough to care for the individuals who in some way might even be victims of the society, but it is also necessary to bring about the needed societal and institutional changes to enhance respect for life, especially for those whose lives are most precarious. Connected with this whole attitude of social change is also an attempt to act as advocates for the poor, the elderly and the less fortunate. Here, too, it is fitting that the Church should take upon itself this role of advocacy because the Gospel reminds us that the poor and the little ones who have no one else to protect them have in some way always been the privileged people in God's kingdom.[26]

The final part of this chapter will consider the crucial question for the Church as such, or groups within the Church or one particular Church group support a partural reform of institutions. For example, should the CHurch or one particular Church group support a particular piece of legislation, such as a specific health care bill, or a particular strategy, such as court-ordered busing to achieve integration of schools. The nub of the problem can be stated quite simply. On the one hand, response to the Gospel includes the need for a change of social structures, but on specific matters there are so many factors that enter into the final judgment that one cannot know with absolute certitude what is the proper Christian response.[27]

The Roman Catholic tradition, to its great credit in my judgment, has always emphasized that our moral judgments are not based only on the Gospel but also take account of all other forms of wisdom and knowledge available to human reason including the data of the sciences. However, in the light of all these other considerations, Christians might arrive at various conclusions about the proper Christian response to very complex questions. On specific questions, absolute certitude cannot be reached or the fear of error cannot be avoided because of the very complexity of the reality itself. In light of this, the question arises: can and should the Church as such speak out? Is it possible to speak in the name of the Gospel when so many factors other than the Gospel are involved? Can one speak in the name of the whole Church when individual members are free in conscience to disagree with such a teaching? On the other hand, if the Church keeps silent does it merely accept and acquiesce in the status quo?

At times and on some issues I believe that the Church as a whole through its leaders (the hierarchical magisterium in the Roman Catholic Church) or through assemblies somewhat representative of the Church (councils, synods, convocations) can and should speak out on specific issues. However, there are some very important considerations that must guide the Church in so doing. First, in speaking out on such issues all the relevant data must be mastered. There is no substitute for knowing the facts and doing one's homework. Too often Church people are accused of being do-gooders who really do not know all the details of the reality being considered. Second, it is impossible for the Church either through the hierarchical magisterium or through broader assemblies to speak out on all the issues, if only because the Church does not and cannot have readily accessible the expertise necessary to master the facts and data involved in all the matters of legislation facing our society. Consequently, there must be a discernment process by which the more important moral and societal issues are discovered since the Church cannot speak on all these issues. Third, if after due deliberation and consideration of all the relevant data, the Church does speak out it must be recognized that dissent or disagreement by individual members of the Church is possible. One cannot take away the rightful freedom of the believer on these issues because in the midst of such complexity it is impossible to say that there is only one Gospel way of dealing with the question. However, the individual should give great importance to such Church statements.

There are also other ways in which the Church can and should become involved in such specific issues. Obviously, the individual Christian on the basis of Christian convictions can work for specific legislation or institutional changes of structure. In addition, there is much room for smaller groups within the Church to work for very specific goals. Unfortunately in the United States there has not been much emphasis on these smaller groups or communities within the Church. In other countries the phenomenon of small communities living a very intense Christian life and working for specific social and political change is much more common.[28] However, there are within the Church in the United States some smaller groups such as Justice and

Peace Commissions, or Catholic Charities or other iden-
tifiable groups who can and should work for very specific social changes.

In the last few years there have been a number of
different examples of this type of Church involvement
in specific moral questions affecting public policy. One
can think of the war in southeast Asia, the question of
court-ordered busing to achieve racial integration in the
schools and unionization of farm workers. Here are
three examples of very specific and important questions
on which individual Christians might be able to disagree, but on which the Church as a whole or smaller
groups within the Church did speak out.

A contemporary question concerns the attempt by the
Roman Catholic bishops to work for a constitutional
amendment prohibiting abortion. No one should deny
that abortion constitutes a very significant moral problem in our society. Likewise, in our pluralistic society it is
important that Catholic religious leaders and other religious leaders and people be free to work for those social
changes which they believe to be in the best interest of
the human community.

We are not now talking about the teaching of
the hierarchical magisterium condemning direct
abortion from the moment of conception. Even on
the moral issue dissent remains a possibility for the
loyal Roman Catholic because of the very complexity
of the question and lack of the certitude in determining
when human life begins and how to solve conflict situations. However, the possibility of dissent does not mean
that one should dissent. A Roman Catholic must pay
significant attention to the teaching of the hierarchical
magisterium. Obviously that teaching should strive to be
as credible as it possibly can. In my judgment human life
is present from very early in the pregnancy (the four-

teenth to twenty-first day), and abortion after that time is justified only for the sake of another life or a value commensurate with life. But now our consideration involves only the legal question of abortion.

This discussion raises the question of the relationship between civil law and morality.[29] An older Catholic view saw the civil law as enforcing the natural law although at times a lesser evil could be tolerated in order to avoid a greater evil. The Declaration on Religious Liberty of the Second Vatican Council proposes a changed understanding of civil law: "For the rest, the usages of society are to be the usages of freedom in their full range. This requires that the freedom of man be respected as far as possible and curtailed only when and insofar as necessary" (par. n. 7). The state and law must respect the freedom of people as much as possible and interfere only when required by public order—public order is distinct from the broader concept of the common good and embraces the threefold reality of an order of justice, an order of peace and an order of public morality.[30]

Since Catholic hierarchical teaching holds that the fetus is a human being and a weak human being in need of protection, one could rightly argue that there should be a law prohibiting abortion and thereby upholding the rights of the fetus. However, one could also argue that other realities must be taken into consideration in determining what the law should be. The law must be equitable, so that if one concludes that an abortion law favors the rich and unduly puts a burden on the poor, then perhaps there should be no law. Laws must also be enforceable, but some point to great numbers of clandestine or illegal abortions wherever abortions are prohibited, thus indicating that the law cannot be enforced. Also in a pluralistic society one must at least consider the rights of others who do not believe that abortion kills a human being. Finally, law-making itself can be a very pragmatic enterprise. Before the Supreme Court ruling in January 1973, a legislator totally opposed to abortion might very well have come to the conclusion of working for a moderate law which would allow some abortions or abortion up to a certain time, if there seemed to be no chance of enacting a restrictive law. Such a legislator might reasonably have concluded that a modified law against abortion is better than no law at all.

All the above factors concerned with the meaning of law in a pluralistic society indicate that one could come to the conclusion that there should be a restrictive abortion law or a modified law or even no law at all against abortion even though one firmly believes that the fetus is a living human being. As a matter of fact there were Roman Catholics who espoused all these opinions—a restrictive law, a moderate law or no law at all. My own opinion opted for some type of moderate law.

In January 1973, the Supreme Court ruled that no law should be made concerning abortion in the first trimester of pregnancy; in the second trimester laws could be made only for the sake of the health of the mother; only in the third trimester can the states make laws to protect the fetus, but abortion must still be permitted to save the life and health of the mother.[31] Since that time many people in our society including the U.S. Roman Catholic bishops have been working for a constitutional amendment which would overturn the Court's decision and protect the fetus.

I personally am opposed to working for a constitutional amendment for a number of different reasons. First, I can understand why the Court came to its decision. There are many problems and difficulties in the reasoning employed by the Court; but it seems that, given the present situation, the Court probably had no other alternative than to come to the conclusion it did. Both a contemporary Catholic theology and the Court accept the basic principle of jurisprudence that freedom should be enhanced as much as possible and constrained only when and insofar as necessary. On the question of abortion the people in the United States are quite divided. Perhaps one could maintain that almost half the people are against abortion, but at the very least it seems that over half the people favor abortion at least in some circumstances. In the light of this situation and applying the principle that in doubt the presumption goes to the freedom of the individual, one can see why the final conclusion of the Court was reached. I am not ecstatic about the situation in this country according to which a great number of people do not believe the fetus is a human being, but this is the reality. I wish the reality were otherwise, but in the light of the situation I understand why the Court came to its conclusion. Second, as already mentioned, I would have favored some type of modified law and not a totally restrictive law as is often proposed by backers of a constitutional amendment.

Third, efforts to amend the Constitution in my judgment will not be successful. Why? The amendment preferred by most backers of the right to life simply states that the fetus has all the rights of a human person. But a problem arises as to when the fetus has these rights. If it is determined that the rights begin at the moment of fertilization as Roman Catholic hierarchical teaching and practice would maintain, this could make the IUD unconstitutional. Obviously the vast majority of people in the United States would not be in favor of that. On the other hand, if one proposed that individual human life begins at the second or third week or the eighth or tenth week, there would be many who would not accept that understanding. Yes, there are many people—

although the latest polls indicate not a majority—who are opposed to the decision by the Court, but they will never be able to agree on the time when the fetus becomes an individual human being with all the rights of a person.

The second type of amendment is often referred to as a states' rights amendment because it would allow the individual states to make laws against abortion. There are two problems that come to my mind with such an approach. First, it seems that for many people states' rights has been a way of trying to avoid some of the progressive social justice enactments that have taken place in the United States in the last few decades. I would not like to see these enactments threatened in any way. Second, a states' rights amendment ultimately will not do much to cut down on the number of abortions. Before the decision of the Supreme Court, a number of states did permit abortion. This would obviously happen again so that people would come to these states from other states, and the total number of abortions would not be appreciably reduced. In my judgment, consequently, attempts to amend the Constitution are futile.

Is there nothing, then, that one can do? There are many forms of education and consciousness-raising that the Roman Catholic Church as a whole and individual groups within the Church can do. In addition, I would propose one very practical and effective approach. At the present time a collection is taken up in all Catholic Churches for Respect Life Week. I propose that with the money from this collection an advertisement be taken out in the twenty or twenty-five largest newspapers in the United States indicating that the people who contributed to this collection believe that the fetus is a human being. As a consequence of this belief they have contributed money to insure that any woman who is pregnant will have the economic, medical, sociological, and psychological and whatever other help is necessary to bring her child to term. In addition, if necessary, help will be given to the mother in caring for the child, or other provisions will be made for the care of child if the mother so wishes. Obviously there will be some difficulties in trying to make this plan practical, but there are already many existing Catholic agencies throughout the country under the aegis of Catholic Charities which would be able to provide these services. Also many volunteers would be attracted to these endeavors. Such an approach provides a creative and positive response to the problem as it exists at the present time. In my judgment much more good could come from such a program than from channeling so much time and effort into attempting to amend the Constitution.

The specific question of abortion laws well illustrates the type of problem created when the Church is faced with very specific questions about what should be done in our society. Here too, there certainly is a place for smaller groups within the Church to work for what they think is right and proper. Even the hierarchical Church can become involved in efforts to arrive at specific legislation but should always do so with the recognition that other members of the Church might disagree. However, in this particular case I would prefer if the American bishops channeled their efforts into the positive approach I outlined above and did not become involved in working for a constitutional amendment.

Respect for life has become an often used slogan in our society. This chapter has attempted to study in a more reflective way the basis and meaning of respect for life and to indicate its implications as well as the nuances that have entered into the understanding and application of respect for life. Finally, strategies or ways for the Church, smaller groups within the Church or individual Christians to make respect for life more present in our society have been discussed and evaluated.

NOTES

1. Daniel Callahan, "The Sanctity of Life," in *Updating Life and Death,* de Donald R. Cutler (Boston: Beacon Press, 1969), pp. 181–230; James M. Gustafson and Henry K. Beecher, "Commentary," in *Updating Life and Death,* pp. 230-242.

2. Marcellinus Zalba, *Theologiae Moralis Summa,* vol. II: *Tractatus de Mandatis Dei et Ecclesiae* (Madrid: Biblioteca de Autores Cristianos, 1953), pp. 256ff.

3. E.g., William E. May, "What Makes a Human Being to be a Being of Moral Worth?" *The Thomist* 40 (1976): 416-443.

4. Jacques Maritain, *Man and the State* (Chicago: University of Chicago Press, Phoenix Books, 1956), p. 77.

5. *Summa Theologiae,* I ^{a}, Prologue.

6. Karl Barth had difficulty in acknowledging any distinction between directly intending the death of another and allowing the person to die. See his *Church Dogmatics* III, 4: 425ff. (Edinburgh: Clark, 1961).

7. Daniel A. Cronin, *The Moral Law in Regard to the Ordinary and Extraordinary Means of Conserving Human Life* (Rome: Pontifical Gregorian University, 1956), p. 128.

8. The American Catholic bishops have tried to emphasize all the implications of respect for life. See *Respect Life Program 1973,* published by the United States Catholic Conference and also the February 1976 statement of the Administrative Board of the United States Catholic Conference, "Political Responsibility," *Origins: N.C. Documentary Service* 5 no. 36 (February 26, 1976): 566-570. However, in practice there appears to be some schizophrenia. Only in the area of abortion have the bishops tried to organize people to bring about a pro-life legislative program ("Pastoral Plan for Pro-Life Activities," National Conference of Catholic Bishops, November 20, 1975, published in pamphlet form by the United States Catholic Conference). Also after interviews with the presidential candidates in the fall of 1976 the president of the National Conference of Catholic Bishops

talked about the candidates almost exclusively in terms of abortion, although these statements were later clarified.

9. Charles E. Curran, *New Perspectives in Moral Theology* (Notre Dame, Ind.: University of Notre Dame Press, 1976), pp. 190ff.

10. Joseph F. Donceel, "Abortion: Mediate or Immediate Animation," *Continuum* 5 (1967): 167-171; Donceel, "A Liberal Catholic View," in *Abortion in a Changing World*, ed. Robert E. Hall (New York: Columbia University Press, 1970), I: 39-45; Donceel, "Immediate Animation and Delayed Hominization," *Theological Studies* 31 (1970): 76-105. For a contrary viewpoint which explains Aquinas's teaching on the basis of the faulty biological knowledge of his time, see Germain Grisez, *Abortion: The Myths, the Realities and the Arguments* (New York and Cleveland: Corpus Books, 1970), p. 283.

11. Grisez, *Abortion*, pp. 273ff.

12. Paul Ramsey, "The Morality of Abortion," in Edward Shils et al., *Life or Death: Ethics and Options* (Seattle: University of Washington Press, 1968), pp. 71ff.

13. Petrus Lombardus, *Libri IV Sententiarum*, lib. 3, dist. 33, cap. 1.

14. Hermenegildus Lio, *Estne Obligatio Justitiae Subvenire Miseris?* (Rome: Desclee, 1957), pp. 27, 28.

15. Here I am following the work and the conclusions proposed by Lio. For a summary of the conclusions of his historical study, see Lio, pp. 107, 108. Lio here differs somewhat from the conclusions downplaying the reality of justice proposed by Odon Lottin, "La nature du devoir de l'aumône chez les prédécesseurs de Saint Thomas d'Aquin," *Ephemerides Theologicae Lovanienses* 15 (1938): 613-624. This study is also incorporated into Lottin's major work, *Psychologie et Morale au XIIe et XIIIe siècle* (Louvain: Abbaye du Mont César, 1949, III-1: 299-313.

16. Lio, *Estne Obligatio*, pp. 101-108. Lio insinuates (pp. 107, 211) that it might be in keeping with Thomistic thinking to see the obligation to give one's superfluous goods to the poor as related to distributive justice. For an opinion seeing the obligation even in Thomas in terms of legal justice, see L. Bouvier, *Le précepte del l'aumône chez saint Thomas d'Aquin*, (Montreal: Collegium Immaculatae Conceptionis, 1935), pp. 183ff. For a summary of the literature and a defense of the more generally accepted opinion that there is no obligation in justice but only in charity, see Marcellino Zalba, "El motivo de la limosna," *Fomento Social* 3 (1948): 421-426.

17. Pope Leo XIII, *Rerum Novarum*, in *Acta Sanctae Sedis* 23 (1890-1891): 651. For a readily available English translation, see *Rerum Novarum*, par. n. 22 in *The Church Speaks to the Modern World: The Social Teachings of Leo XIII*. ed. Etienne Gilson (Garden City, N.Y.: Doubleday Image Book, 1954), pp. 217, 218.

18. John A. Ryan, *A Living Wage* (New York: Macmillan, 1906).

19. A summary of Ryan's reasoning may be found in his *Distributive Justice* (New York: Macmillan, 1916), pp. 323-399.

20. Gene Outka, "Social Justice and Equal Access to Health Care," *The Journal of Religious Ethics* 2 (1974): 11-32.

21. For a study of the papal social teaching which is more cognizant of development in that teaching than many other studies, see Richard L. Camp, *The Papal Ideology of Social Reform: A Study in Historical Development* (Leiden: E. J. Brill, 1969).

22. *Rerum Novarum, Acta Sanctae Sedis* 23 (1890-1891): 643-655; Gilson, par. nn. 4-31.

23. *Populorum Progressio, Acta Apostolicae Sedis* 59 (1967): 268-278. For an English version of this and other official Church documents on the social question since 1960, see *The Gospel of Peace and Justice: Catholic Social Teaching since Pope John,* presented by Joseph Gremillion (Maryknoll, N.Y.: Orbis Books, 1976).

24. For a more minute analysis of the development in the hierarchical teaching on the question of private property, see J. Diez-Alegria, "La lettura del magistero pontificio in materia sociale alla luce del suo sviluppo storico," in *Magistero et Morale: Atti del 3° congresso nazionale dei moralisti* (Bologna: Edizioni Dehoniane, 1970), pp. 211-256.

25. Christian personalism is often associated with the theories of Emmanuel Mounier. See Eileen Cantin, *Mounier: A Personalist View of History* (New York: Paulist Press, 1973). Christian personalism in the United States is often associated with Dorothy Day and the Catholic Worker Movement as well as with Paul Hanly Furfey; see David J. O'Brien, *American Catholics and Social Reform: The New Deal Years* (New York: Oxford University Press, 1968), pp. 182-211.

26. The National Conference of Catholic Charities has recognized the importance of its own functioning as an advocate for the poor; see *Towards a Renewed Catholic Charities Movement* (Washington: National Conference of Catholic Charities, 1971).

27. I have developed this question in greater depth in my article "Theological Reflections on the Social Mission of the Church," in *The Social Mission of the Church: A Theological Reflection,* ed. Edward J. Ryle (Washington, D.C.: The National Catholic School of Social Service, the Catholic University of America, 1972), pp. 31-54.

28. See, for example, "Les communautes nouvelles," in *Le Supplément* no. 98 (September, 1971): 263-350; also *Concilium,* no. 84 (April 1973) and no. 96 (June 1974).

29. For an in depth discussion of this question, see my *Ongoing Revision: Studies in Moral Theology* (Notre Dame, Ind.: Fides Publishes, 1975), pp. 107-143.

30. This teaching is found in paragraph seven of the Declaration

on Religious Freedom. For a succinct explanation of the judicial ramifications, see footnotes 20 and 21, pp. 686 and 687 of *The Documents of Vatican II*, ed. Walter M. Abbott (New York: Guild Press, 1966). The footnotes to the Declaration on Religious Freedom which are not in italics are not official footnotes but comments made by John Courtney Murray.

31. Supreme Court of the United States, *Roe et al.* v. *Wade* (Slip Opinion), pp. 47, 48.

Index